ENIGMAS OF HISTORY

Also by Hugh Ross Williamson

HUGH ROSS WILLIAMSON

Enigmas of History

London
MICHAEL JOSEPH

First published by
MICHAEL JOSEPH LTD
26 Bloomsbury Street,
*London, W.C.*1
MARCH 1957
SECOND IMPRESSION APRIL 1957

Set and printed in Great Britain by Tonbridge Printers Ltd,
Peach Hall Works, Tonbridge, Kent, in Baskerville eleven
on thirteen point, on paper made by Henry Bruce at Currie,
Midlothian, and bound by James Burn at Esher, Surrey

To KENNETH ADAM

CONTENTS

Tôt ou tard, tout se scait

MAINTENON

Men wiser and more learned than I have discovered in history a plot, a rhythm, a predetermined pattern. I can see only one emergency following upon another as wave follows upon wave, only one great fact with respect to which, since it is unique, there can be no generalizations, only one safe rule for the historian: that he should recognize in the development of human destinies the play of the contingent and the unforeseen.

H. A. L. FISHER

FOREWORD

THE immemorial instinct of mankind 'to tell sad stories of the death of kings' is no longer enough for the historian. Nowadays he has to know the texture of the shroud and its cost per foot in terms of a fluctuating shilling linked to the export price of wool. The President of the Historical Association, in his Jubilee Address, in 1956, recalled the remark of the Cambridge College porter: 'The men going in and out of this gate used to be gentlemen; now they are only scholars.' One sees what the porter meant. And anything can happen when history ceases to be a gentle hobby.

What in fact has happened Dr Butterfield hinted in that same address, when he said, 'The early part of the twentieth century saw historians building up their institutional organization. Together with the development of more serious teaching in schools and universities, this established history as a profession and a vested interest.'

Thus he defined accurately (though not perhaps intentionally) the nature of the catastrophe which today has overtaken historical writing. It has become a vested interest. Text-books and examinations, prestige and preferments, degrees and doctorates, royalties and emoluments are now involved in its orthodoxies. It must be a 'science'; it must have a 'method'; it must flourish 'facts'; it must announce 'conclusions.'

11

But, as I have been perhaps over-pertinacious in pointing out, it can unfortunately do none of these things. 'History' can record only a millionth part of the 'facts,' is unable, in consequence, to draw any 'conclusions' which can rightly be termed 'scientific' and has no 'method' other than that which applies equally to any form of investigation, from designing an aeroplane to solving a murder—that is to say, finding out as much as possible, expressing and using that knowledge honestly, testing the conclusions and admitting that, at any moment, something new may be discovered which will invalidate the tentative solution.

I shall not be so tedious as to repeat here the theory of history which I have already elaborated on more than one occasion; but I feel bound, in charity, to warn any of the young into whose hands either this book or its predecessor *Historical Whodunits* may fall that they should on no account incorporate my conclusions in their examination answers. To do so would be to ensure very low marks, if not actual failure. It is not that what I have written is not, to the best of my knowledge, research and belief, as near the truth as it is possible to get. It is that, *if* it is true, it reduces most of the vested interest text-books to absurdity; and this, as it would have considerable economic repercussions, could never be allowed.

If for example it is impossible to be certain of a simple fact like the identity of the executioner of Charles I, why should anyone suppose it possible to write an authoritative assessment of an extremely complicated subject like the origin of the Civil War? If Queen Victoria ought not to have succeeded to the Throne until 1849, what happens to learned treatises

12

on the constitutional development of the Cabinet under Melbourne? If Mary Tudor, who was the undoubted daughter of Henry VIII, was right in believing that her 'half-sister' Elizabeth was not—and she was presumably in a better position to assess it than was Mr Froude or even Professor Pollard—what reliance can be based on those who attribute Elizabeth's outlook to her inheritance from her Royal father? And so on.

For myself, it does not 'matter' one way or the other, any more than it 'matters' whether Henry VII murdered the Princes in the Tower, whether Cecil organized the Gunpowder Plot, whether William Rufus was a pagan sacrificial victim or whether Queen Elizabeth was an accessory before the fact in the murder of Amy Robsart. I think that all these things are so, because all the evidence I have been able to discover points relentlessly to those conclusions. But obviously, on my own theory of history, I may be wrong. If I am, no great harm is done. I have tried my best to find out what happened to certain people and to discover what kind of people they were and failed. And even if I am right, it is no more than a story which, perhaps, later writers will be able to fill in in a little more detail.

But, the effect on the vested interest of my being right would be shattering. It would mean that the books and the examination papers would all have to be rewritten and reset. It would mean more importantly the collapse of all those pretensions to 'scientific scholarship'; for there really would be little more point in having Chairs of History than Chairs of Memoir-Writing or Chairs of Detection or, more pertinently, Chairs of Propaganda.

It is always difficult to find a simple example to illustrate a theory, but it so happens that, in a recent

review in *The Times Literary Supplement* of a book on the
Dead Sea Scrolls, there appeared a passage which
explains my point with exactitude. The reviewer wrote
that the author of the book 'claims that, because the
first cave showed no signs of occupation after A.D. 70,
all the documents found in it must have been written
and deposited there before that date. This, however,
clashes with the only *firm historical allusion* in this group
of texts . . . the statement in the commentary on
Habakkuk that the enemy sacrificed to their standards.
. . . The only occasion on which the Romans are *known*
to have sacrificed to (as distinct from venerated) their
standards was in the autumn of A.D. 70 when the Roman
soldiers forced their way into the precincts of the
Temple at Jerusalem. To say that this must refer to
some other unknown occasion is to *adopt a method* by
which anything may be proved of anything.' (My
italics.)

The reviewer thus reveals the assumptions under-
lying academic history. The first is that everything that
happened is recorded—rather as a full list of all
coming-out dances appears in *The Times* newspaper.
The second is that, if a thing is not recorded, it cannot,
by 'historical method' be presumed to have happened.
The third is that, if a thing is recorded, it is both accurate
and unique and must be the factor given precedence in
any investigation.

The absurdity of these axioms is, I should have
thought, self-evident; yet on their acceptance all the
propositions of academic history rest. In this particular
case there is no reason whatever to suppose that the
recorded instance in A.D. 70 of the Romans sacrificing
to their standards is the only occasion on which it

happened; nor is there any reason to suppose that 'veneration,' as a ritual, necessarily excluded 'sacrifice' merely because it was not reported. For all anyone knows, such sacrifices may have been a conventional annual or even monthly occurrence. The incident in Jerusalem has thus no bearing on the dating of the cave. That must be considered in the light of other evidence; and if such evidence is sufficient to give a reasonable certainty that the cave was deserted at the time of the Jerusalem episode and that, therefore, the already written Scrolls cannot refer to it, the only correct proceeding is that which the author has followed—postulate an 'unknown' (i.e. formally un-recorded or so far undiscovered) occasion.

But this, cries the reviewer in alarm, voicing the panic of all academic historians, is 'to adopt a method by which anything may be proved of anything.' If the overstatement be put in the terms that 'nothing can be *proved* from documentary evidence' he is perfectly right. Nothing can. That is my point. 'Documentary evidence' alone is worthless, simply because what on any point has survived cannot be presumed to be the total documentary evidence and therefore cannot be properly evaluated, even supposing it be genuine and accurate, (which, in cases of critical and disputed events, it often is not). 'History' cannot be more, when it is honest, than an enquiry into possibilities; and 'documentary evidence' is only one, and not the most important, of its components.

I will not pursue the matter further except in self-defence to acquaint the non-academic reader with one line of attack which has been directed against my innocent enquiries. Academics, defending their vested interest, occasionally find that they have to admit that their official version of history has been shaken. The evidence is too strong to ignore, but, they say, people of my kind go too far in the opposite direction. The favourite phrase is 'the swing of the pendulum.' The Gunpowder Plot, for instance, may not be all that S. R. Gardiner thought it was, but it is ridiculous to suppose that it is all I think it is. The pendulum has swung too far.

Seldom has an analogy been more misleading. If a detective enquiry exonerated from murder one suspect, would anyone claim that Scotland Yard should be on its guard lest the swing of the pendulum might lead them to suspect someone else? If the alleged motives of A have been successfully disproved, must we guard against the swing of the pendulum leading us to enquire into the possible motives of B?

The story of the Emperor's New Clothes is pertinent. The child's perception that the Emperor was in fact unclothed must have been very galling to the tailors, who had published accounts of the clothes which they had made and which they said he was wearing. Did they explain, in self-defence: 'Well, we agree that the Emperor's clothes are not altogether like those we originally described to you; but you will notice that the coat he has on, although not perhaps a long coat, in the proper meaning of the word long, cannot correctly be described as a short coat either. There have been far shorter coats. And if the breeches are not scarlet silk, they seem to have an appearance of red in the strong sunlight and the sheen is not unlike that of silk?'

Such a reaction on the part of a vested interest, whether of tailors or of dons, is not only comprehensible but even disarming; and the child would have to be very childish indeed if he expected anything else from them, especially as, in the words of a writer in *The Times* newspaper in the November of 1956, 'in the best-informed Senior Common and Combination Rooms . . . . . what was taught to little Arthur still in essentials holds water.'

On the other hand, he might hope that some of the disinterested spectators in the crowd would see, if not the King's nakedness, at least the tailors' point in denying it. But that I must leave to my readers . . .

Four of the pieces in this book are based upon broadcasts I made in my third series of *Historical Whodunits*—the executioner of Charles I, the affair of Sir John Fenwick, the Man in the Iron Mask and the Diamond Necklace. As the choice of these subjects was in answer to requests from listeners, I may be permitted to say that I cannot claim the kind of background knowledge for the two famous French mysteries that I have for the English, though I am delighted to be able to give Lord Quickswood's brilliant theory about 'the Mask' a more permanent form than the spoken word.

HUGH ROSS WILLIAMSON

London,
November, 1956

I

THE WIVES
OF KING GEORGE IV

[i] Question and Answer 1956

WHEN I was asked to investigate more dark corners of history, I decided to use the occasion to probe what lay behind the trial of Caroline, Queen of George IV. This attempt of the King to divorce his wife in 1820 brought England to the verge of revolution. It led, among other things, to the formation of the modern police force and to the founding of the magazine, *John Bull*. It contained psychological puzzles, especially as regards the characters of George and Caroline, for George seemed altogether too stupid and vindictive and Caroline too indiscreet and at the same time too innocent. And the great trial, which was European news less than a century and a half ago, had been so completely forgotten that I was able to buy a report of it—1,100 pages of small print—for a mere four shillings.

Having read the available printed sources, I went to manuscripts. At the Public Record Office, I asked for material on Queen Caroline and was duly brought a folder marked HO 126/3 which contained many letters, documents and official copies of State papers connected with the case. There was, however, one odd thing about the folder. The list of documents which it was said to contain did not tally with the documents which it did in fact contain.

As it was marked 126/3, I thought it might be worth investigating 126/1 and 126/2, but the catalogue on the open shelves bore no reference to the whereabouts of these bundles. More by good luck than good management, I was able to see a catalogue not generally accessible to the public which listed the elusive 1 and 2 thus:

1. Transferred to Buckingham Palace
   for incorporation in the Royal Archives
   at Windsor in July 1935   1 chest
2. As above   1 bundle

The mystery suddenly became modern, though the question why the removal had been made, interesting as it was, took for the moment second place to the historian's natural annoyance that the Public Record Office could be thus raided and a chestful of once-public documents put beyond the researcher's reach. As it seemed to involve a matter of principle which, if continued, could lead to even more falsification—or, at least, falsification at a different level—than is, by definition, inherent in 'history,' I wrote a short letter to the Press, stating the facts.

Mr Montgomery Hyde, M.P., the authority on George IV's Foreign Secretary, Castlereagh (who was vitally concerned in the matter of Queen Caroline) saw my letter and was good enough to table a question in the House of Commons. The result, as reported in *Hansard* for February 2, 1956, I quote in full so that the reader may form his own judgment.

Public Record Office
(Removal of Documents)

Mr Speaker: Mr David Jones—Question No. 59.

MR HYDE: On a point of order. You have not called Question 58, which is in my name, Mr Speaker.

MR SPEAKER: I understood that the hon. Member's Question was withdrawn.

MR HYDE: It was not.

MR SPEAKER: Mr David Jones.

MR HYDE: Further to that point of order. I asked the Table to withdraw the Question if it were not reached.

MR SPEAKER: The hon. Member ought not to give such hypothetical instructions. Mr David Jones.

MR HYDE: Further to that point of order, Mr Speaker, am I not right in saying that it is customary to ask the Table to withdraw a Question if it is not reached?

MR SPEAKER: I understand the custom has grown up for a Member to ask for his Question to be withdrawn if it is not reached, but I understood the hon. Gentleman's Question was definitely withdrawn.

MR HYDE: No, Sir, only if it were not reached. I asked that in that event it should be put off until next Thursday.

MR SPEAKER: Mr Hyde.

58. Mr Hyde asked the Secretary to the Treasury why two bundles of documents relating to Queen Caroline, wife of King George IV, covering the years 1804 to 1820, have been removed from the Public Record Office; and where they are now located and whether they can be seen by students.

MR H. BROOKE: The documents concerned were, on examination in 1935, considered to be not public records or State papers but part of the Sovereign's private family archives. They were accordingly transferred, with the written authority of the then Master of the Rolls and the then Secretary of State for the

Home Department, from the Public Record Office to the Royal Archives at Windsor, where they now remain and where, it is understood, they are not open to inspection.

MR HYDE: Is my right hon. Friend aware that these papers arrived at the Public Record Office over a hundred years ago from the old State Paper Office, and that they remained there for the best part of a century, where they were seen by the public? Will he make it clear now that they were eventually transferred to Windsor, not on account of the nature of their contents but because of their character?

MR BROOKE: My information is that they were transferred because of their private nature.

There is no doubt that the answers are strictly true. But the question remains as to what is meant by 'private family archives' in such a matter as the relationship between King George IV and Queen Caroline which was the pivot of the political and constitutional history of England for twenty years. Enough is known about the characters of George and Caroline to make any further revelations on that score irrelevant; and the attempt of George IV to divorce Queen Caroline can only be called a private family matter if the same description is allowed to the attempt of Henry VIII to divorce Queen Catherine.

By this time, the enigma of 1820 was in my mind taking second place to the enigma of 1935, and eventually, puzzling over it, the possible solution of the one gave the clue to the probable solution of the other. I was convinced, by what I had now read, that Caroline had been 'framed' by George, at least as far as the adultery charge went; and the manner in which it was done

showed that the King was going to lengths so extraordinary that they must have been dictated by a relentless personal imperative. Was the reason that, as he was
married privately to Maria Fitzherbert (who was by
the Pope, by the King and by the Royal Family, as well
as by Mrs Fitzherbert herself, considered his only true
wife) he never considered Caroline as his wife at all?
Certainly he never forgave her her celebrated remark
at the time of the trial that she had only committed
adultery once and that was with the husband of Mrs
Fitzherbert. And though, at the time of her trial, he was
no longer living with her but was the victim of many
mistresses, she remained the only woman he loved and
he died and was buried with her miniature round his
neck. Was it not possible that for this reason he was
determined that, cost what it might, no other woman
should share his throne?

I had, up to this point, considered the Fitzherbert
marriage as one among several factors to be taken into
account; but it was the date—1935—of the removal of
the chest of papers to Windsor that suddenly made me
see its unique importance. For we know that, according
to J. G. Lockhart's official life of the then Archbishop
of Canterbury, Cosmo Gordon Lang, that in 1935 King
George V had a 'long and intimate' conversation with
the Archbishop about the attachment of the Prince of
Wales to Mrs Simpson. It was not many months later
that the question of Edward VIII's morganatic marriage
was mooted; and it was possible that George IV's
marriage to Mrs Fitzherbert had received such emphasis
in the Caroline papers that George V, feeling as he did
about his son's love for Mrs Simpson, considered that
the public interest was best served by their removal to

the privacy of the Windsor archives, where references to an unwelcome precedent could, if necessary, be destroyed at leisure.

There had already been, on Mrs Fitzherbert's death, a wholesale destruction by the Crown of papers in her possession, from which only the marriage certificate and one or two other documents necessary to vindicate her character and status had survived in the safety of Coutts' Bank.

There can be, I think, no doubt that Mrs Fitzherbert knew the truth about many relationships at the court of George IV of which today we have no clue left. To Caroline she was always a friend and during the time of the Queen's trial, she went to Paris so that there was no chance of her being impounded as a witness. For she was a woman of the most unbending principles and one to whom the committing of perjury was inconceivable.

But there is one curious fact which has survived the general destruction, though not—as far as can be discovered—the documentary proof of it. Her son-in-law, George Dawson-Damer has left on record a remark she made long after the people concerned were dead:

'Princess of Wales (Caroline) married to Prince Louis. Could have bastardized Princess Charlotte. Compounded with the mother—Lord Loughborough by George III's commands. She saw Princess Charlotte who implored her. A peer still alive, who had been a lover of the Princess of Wales, who implored him to destroy the certificate of marriage to Prince Louis.'

Was it possible that Caroline as well as George was married before their state-marriage to each other?

And, finally, how did all this bear on the true identity of 'William Austin'—the boy whom Caroline adopted and who was officially pronounced to be the son of poor parents, but whom everybody (including George) assumed to be Caroline's own child and whom Caroline swore to James Brougham was the son of the Prince Louis Ferdinand who was killed at Jena in 1806?

William Austin was never separated from Caroline till her death and she made him her heir. He was born during the time that she and George were married and were both living in London and therefore, had the boy been proved to have been her child he would have been 'legally' also George's, under the law that, if the husband was in the Kingdom ('within the four seas') he was presumed to be the father of his wife's children, unless it could be proved that access was impossible or that he was impotent. This surely explains what the Duke of Sussex meant when he told his brother George in 1806 that Caroline's conduct must be investigated since facts had come to light which 'might affect the royal succession.'

And, as 'William Austin' did not die till 1849, the question must have been of more than academic interest in the year 1837 which saw both the death of Mrs Fitzherbert and the accession to the throne of George IV's young niece, Victoria.

The public events, which culminated in the trial and acquittal of Queen Caroline and her subsequent exclusion from Westminster Abbey on the occasion of George IV's coronation, thus lead back to mysteries which were, then and now, altogether hidden from the public, and the probabilities, as far as they can be unravelled, reveal a tension of personal relationships as fascinating as any in history.

George dared not reveal his marriage to Mrs

Fitzherbert (though, at one point he threatened to) for, as
she was a Catholic, he would, under the Act of Settle-
ment, have had to abdicate. Caroline for fear of a
European scandal dared not admit her marriage (if it
existed) to Prince Louis Ferdinand, who visited her in
England when, to cover their relationship, she pretended
in public to be interested in one of his staff. Neither
George nor Caroline, for different reasons, wished the
Royal Commission to establish that William Austin was
Caroline's child—though George believed it and
Caroline behaved as if it were true. George, determined
by some means to get rid of Caroline caused her to be
cited for an act of adultery with an Italian, of which she
was undoubtedly innocent; Caroline, though knowing
that her character would be irrevocably damaged during
the proceedings, insisted on standing her trial, despite
George's offer to her of £50,000 a year to remain out
of England. In the same year as Caroline's trial, he
increased Mrs Fitzherbert's allowance to £10,000 a
year.

In *The Dynasts*, Thomas Hardy has given his Chorus
of Ironic Spirits the well-known lines on the doubly-
married and monotonously unfaithful King:

A wife of the body, a wife of the mind:
A wife somewhat frowsy, a wife too refined—
Could the twain but grow one and no other dames be,
No husband in Europe more faithful than he!

Though this is misleading in its simplicity, any attempt
to unravel the historical complexity must start with the
inter-relation of the two marriages.

[ii] Maria Fitzherbert

Maria Anne Smythe was born in 1756, the daughter of an old Catholic family who had sacrificed everything for the Stuarts. She was twice widowed before she was twenty-five; her second husband, Thomas Fitzherbert of Swynnerton, by whose name she is known in history, was the twenty-fifth Lord of the Manor of Norbury, in direct male line from the reign of Henry I, which gave the family 'an antiquity which made most of the English nobility seem mushrooms.'

When in 1783 the Prince of Wales, four years her junior, first saw her riding in her carriage in the Park, the 'widow Fitzherbert' was accounted one of the beauties of London and George was immediately captivated. Nevertheless, she resisted all his advances until the day when, to quote Lord Stourton's *Narrative*, she met 'a species of attack so unprecedented and alarming as to shake her resolution. . . . Keate the surgeon, Lord Onslow, Lord Southampton and Mr Edward Bouverie arrived at her house in the utmost consternation, informing her that the life of the Prince was in imminent danger —that he had stabbed himself—and that only *her* immediate presence would save him. She resisted, in the most peremptory manner, all their importunities, saying that nothing should induce her to enter Carlton House. She was afterwards brought to share in the alarm but, still fearful of some stratagem derogatory to her reputation, insisted upon some lady of high condition accompanying her as an indispensible condition: the Duchess of Devonshire was selected.

'They four drove from Park Street to Devonshire House and took her along with them. She found the

Prince pale and covered with blood. The sight so over-
powered her faculties that she was deprived almost of
all consciousness. The Prince told her that nothing
would induce him to live unless she promised to become
his wife and permitted him to put a ring round her
finger. I believe a ring from the hand of the Duchess of
Devonshire was used upon this occasion and not one of
his own.

'Mrs Fitzherbert, being asked by me [Lord Stourton]
whether she did not believe that some trick had been
practised and that it was not really the blood of His
Royal Highness, answered in the negative and said that
she had frequently seen the scar . . .

'They returned to Devonshire House. A deposition
of what had occurred was drawn up and signed and
sealed by each one of the party. . . . On the next day
she left the country, sending a letter to Lord Southampton protesting against what had taken place, as not
being then a free agent. She retired to Aix-la-Chapelle
and afterwards to Holland.'

For over a year she remained abroad, the recipient of
constant letters from the Prince. 'The speed of the
couriers,' writes Lord Stourton, 'exciting the suspicion
of the French government, three of them were at different times put into prison. Wrought upon and fearful,
from the past, of the desperation of the Prince, she
consented formally and deliberately to promise she
would never marry any other person; and lastly she was
induced to return to England and to agree to become his
wife on those conditions which satisfied her own conscience, though she could have no legal claim to become
the wife of the Prince of Wales.'

The letter of forty-two pages, dated November 3,

1785, by which George finally prevailed on her is the longest love-letter in the language. In it he made it clear that, since the curious scene in Carlton House, he had always considered himself married to her and he even suggested that his father, the King, was not averse to her becoming his wife. The letter ended: 'Come then, oh come, dearest of wives, best and most sacred of women, come and for ever crown with bliss him who will through life endeavour to convince you by his love and attention of his wishes to be the best of husbands and who will ever remain unto the latest moments of his existence, *unalterably thine.*'

The Prince had already determined to marry no one else and to let the crown descend through the family of his brother, the Duke of York. 'I will never marry,' he had declared. 'My resolution is taken on that subject. I have settled it with Frederick. No, I will never marry. Frederick will marry and the crown will descend to his children.'

Accordingly, George, Prince of Wales and Mrs Fitzherbert were privately married on December 15, 1785, with her brother, Jack Smythe, and her uncle, Henry Errington, as witnesses. The ceremony was performed by the Vicar of Twickenham, according to the marriage service of the Church of England, which was valid in Catholic eyes, though it was, of course, illegal, because it contravened both the Act of Settlement and the Royal Marriage Act. On the one hand, Mrs Fitzherbert was a Catholic; on the other, George lacked the necessary consent of his father, the King.

The first years were happy enough. The honeymoon was spent at Mrs Fitzherbert's villa at Twickenham and when, after Christmas, they returned to Town, though

29

she refused to live at Carlton House, he 'never forgot to go through the form of saying to Mrs Fitzherbert with a most respectful bow: "Madam, may I be allowed the honour of seeing you home in my carriage?" ' She was given the position of honour; all precedence was waived in her favour and the Prince would accept no invitations where she was not given first place. Eventually George, to the extreme displeasure of the King, closed Carlton House and went with his wife to live at Brighton where he built his fantastic Pavilion and she, though living in a small house near, reigned as Queen of it. 'Her own manners,' a diarist noticed, 'ever remained quiet, civil and unperturbed and in the days of her greatest influence she was never accused of using it improperly.' He, on his part, was scrupulous of her honour and dismissed Beau Brummell from his circle of friendship for his bêtise in calling for '*Mistress* Fitzherbert's carriage.'

Unfortunately for them both, the Prince of Wales's mounting debts could be settled only by a grant from Parliament and the now nation-wide rumour of his secret marriage to a Catholic made Pitt, as Chancellor of the Exchequer use his necessity as a lever to prise out the truth. Fox, apparently in good faith, denied the marriage in the House of Commons and, according to Lord Stourton, 'this public degradation of Mrs Fitzherbert so compromised her character and her religion and irritated her feelings that she determined to break off all connection with the Prince, and was only induced to receive him again into her confidence by repeated assurances that Mr Fox had never been authorized to make the declaration.' Sheridan's historic and chivalrous speech in her defence 'affirming that ignorance and

30

vulgar folly alone could have persevered in attempting
to detract from a character upon which truth could fix
no just reproach and which was in reality entitled to the
truest and most general respect,' retrieved the situation
and in the May of 1787 a correspondent recorded that
'the Prince sat at table with Mrs Fitzherbert and all her
particular friends near him. His attention to her has
been more marked lately than usual.'

The separation of the Prince and his wife did not
occur till seven years later when, in the June of 1794,
he had fallen under the influence of the notorious Lady
Jersey. 'From that time' says Stourton, 'she never saw
the Prince and this interruption of their intimacy was
followed by his marriage to Queen Caroline [ten months
later]; brought about, as Mrs Fitzherbert conceived,
under the two-fold influence of the pressure of his debts
on the mind of the Prince and a wish on the part of Lady
Jersey to enlarge the Royal Establishment, in which she
was to have an important situation.'

As the Prince's debts by this time had mounted to
£350,000 and were in the nature of a European scandal,
he was indeed bound to accede to the terms imposed on
him for their settlement—marriage to his first cousin,
Caroline of Brunswick.

To understand the pattern into which this State
marriage falls, it will be most convenient to epitomize
the subsequent relations of George and Maria Fitzherbert. She is said to have fainted when the actual news
of the wedding was brought to her and, in spite of the
fact that George separated from Caroline immediately
an heiress, Princess Charlotte, was born in 1796, Maria
refused to return to him.

The Prince's state of mind, during this second period

of separation, was even more excitable, if possible, than during the first. Three days after the birth of Charlotte, when he had given Caroline her *congé*, he made a will in Mrs Fitzherbert's favour, as passionately written as his unparalleled love-letter ten years earlier. In it he bestowed all his worldly property on 'Maria Fitzherbert, my wife, the wife of my heart and soul' asking that 'my coffin should be taken up and buried next to Hers, wherever she is to be buried and, if she has no objection, that the two inward sides of the two coffins should be taken out and the two coffins then to be soldered together.' Throughout the will, the phrases 'my only true and real Wife,' 'the beloved and adored wife of my heart and soul,' 'my beloved and adored Maria Fitzherbert, my Wife, my Second Self' witness to his feelings. His mother, the Queen, fearing for his health and his reason, wrote to Mrs Fitzherbert, asking for a reconciliation.

By the spring of 1799, George was prepared to make the fact of the Fitzherbert marriage public, no matter what the consequences to everybody involved, and one of the diarists of the time noted: 'Is it that there is a foundation for what is generally whispered, viz., that the Prince of Wales is going to declare his marriage with Mrs Fitzherbert? But what will be proposed for the Princess and her child? Shall we have the old case renewed of Henry VIII and the tables turned on the Protestants?'

In her dilemma, Mrs Fitzherbert appealed to Rome. Father Nassau, one of the staff at the Catholic chapel in Warwick Street, went to the Pope to lay the case before him on the understanding that, if the answer allowed it, she would at once return to her conjugal duties but, if not, she would leave England. The answer from the Vatican confirmed Mrs Fitzherbert's status as the Prince's true and only wife and on the day she rejoined him on June 16, 1800 she gave her famous 'public breakfast to the whole town of London.' The wedding-breakfast (and the world understood it as such) thus took place nearly fifteen years after the marriage.

'She told me,' records Lord Stourton, 'she hardly knew how she could summon resolution to pass that severe ordeal, but she thanked God she had courage to do so. The next eight years were, she said, the happiest of her connection with the Prince. She used to say they were extremely poor, but as merry as crickets and, as proof of their poverty, she told me that once, on their returning to Brighton from London, they mustered their common means and could not raise £5 between them. . . . She added, however, that even this period, the happiest of their lives, was much embittered by the numerous political difficulties which frequently surrounded the Prince, and she particularly alluded to what has been termed 'the Delicate Investigation' [about the parentage of William Austin] in which Queen Caroline and His Royal Highness were concerned.'

By 1809, George had succumbed to a new mistress, Lady Hertford, and Mrs Fitzherbert felt bound to refuse to submit to the treatment she now received when, at George's request, she visited him at the Pavilion. 'Whatever may be thought of me by some individuals,' she wrote to him, 'it is well known Your Royal Highness four and twenty years ago placed me in a situation so nearly connected with your own that I have a claim upon you for protection. I feel I owe it to myself not to be insulted under your roof with impunity. The influence you are now under and the conduct of one of your servants, I am sorry to say, has the appearance of your sanction and support, and renders my situation in your house, situated as I am, impossible any longer to submit to.'

Nevertheless she visited him, at his order, on January 31, 1811, when she pleaded with him to show more kindness to his and Caroline's child, the Princess Charlotte. But in the summer of that year, Lady Hertford persuaded the Prince not to invite her to the great party given to celebrate the inauguration of the Regency (George III having at last gone hopelessly insane) as well as to honour the family of Louis XVI of France—the famous dinner when 'the son of the demented entertained the family of the decapitated.'

Mrs Fitzherbert asked for an audience to receive confirmation of the insult from George herself and the following day she wrote him a letter reminding him that he was 'excluding the person who is not unjustly suspected by the world of possessing in silence unassumed and unsustained a rank given her by yourself above that of any other person present.'

From that day, she rarely saw and never spoke to her husband again, though, nineteen years later in his last illness—she was then seventy-four—she could not resist writing him a letter which began: 'After many repeated struggles with myself, from the apprehension of appearing troublesome or intruding upon Your Majesty after so many years of continual silence, my anxiety respecting Your Majesty has got the better of my scruples.'

George seized the letter, read it with joy and put it under his pillow. But it was too late. Death summoned him before he could summon her. He was buried, as he had wished, with her miniature on his heart.

[iii] Caroline of Brunswick

On August 24, 1794, about two months after Mrs Fitzherbert had left her husband for the first time (on Lady Jersey's account), George III wrote to Pitt from Weymouth: 'I have this morning seen the Prince of Wales, who has acquainted me with his having broken off all connection with Mrs Fitzherbert and his desire of entering into a more creditable line of life by marrying; expressing at the same time that his wish is that my niece, the Princess of Brunswick, may be the person.'

This official version is as far from the truth as official versions tend to be. Caroline of Brunswick herself had no illusions about the matter, and summed it up with: 'I was the victim of Mammon. The Prince of Wales's debts must be paid and poor little I's person was the pretence.' And the Queen, when the Prince discussed the King's insistence on his marriage, told him, with Mrs Fitzherbert in mind: 'It is for you, George, to say whether you can marry the Princess or not.' The combined effect of the King's financial blackmail, Lady Jersey's influence and Mrs Fitzherbert's refusal to return to him made George decide that he could marry the Princess and James Harris, Earl of Malmesbury, went to Brunswick to report.

Malmesbury, meeting Caroline who was nearly twenty-seven, was bound to agree that 'old as she was, her education was not yet completed.' His observations on her were those of an acute and trained diplomatist and accurately portray a character which over the years changed little in essentials.

'Princess Caroline very *gauche* at cards—speaks without thinking—gets too easy—calls the ladies (she never saw) "Mon coeur, ma chère, ma petite." I notice this and reprove it strongly. . . . Princess Caroline very "missish" at supper. I much fear these habits are irrecoverably rooted in her—she is naturally curious, and a gossip—she is quick and observing, and she has a silly pride in finding out everything; she thinks herself particularly acute in discovering likings, and this leads her to the most improper remarks and conversation. . . . On summing up Princess Caroline's character today, it came out to my mind to be that she has quick parts without a sound or distinguishing understanding; that she has a ready conception, but no judgment; caught by the first impression, led by the first impulse; turned away by appearances or *enjouement*; loving to talk and prone to confide and make missish friendships that last twenty-four hours. Some natural but no acquired morality and no strong innate notions of its value and necessity; warm feelings and nothing to counterbalance them; great good humour and much good nature; no appearance of caprice; rather quick and *vive* but not a grain of rancour. From her habits, from the life she was allowed and even compelled to live, forced to dissemble; fond of gossiping and this strengthened greatly by the example of her good mother [George III's sister] who is all curiosity and inquisitiveness, and who has no notion of not gratifying this desire at any price. In short, the Princess, in the hands of a steady and sensible man would probably turn out well; but where it is likely that she will find faults perfectly analogous to her own, she will fail.'

As Malmesbury perceived, she was altogether too like her first cousin whom she was about to marry; and the points on which she differed from him were even more likely to precipitate disaster. 'Argument with the Princess about her toilette. She piques herself on dressing quick; I disapprove this. She maintains her point; I, however, desire Madame Busche to explain to her that the Prince is very delicate and that he expects a long and very careful *toilette de propreté*, of which she has no idea. On the contrary, she neglects it sadly and is offensive from this neglect. Madame Busche executes her commission well and the Princess comes out the next day well washed all over.'

The improvement seems to have been only temporary. Three weeks later, Malmesbury regretfully notes: 'I had conversations with the Princess Caroline on the toilette, on cleanliness and on delicacy of speaking. On these points I endeavoured, as far as was possible for a man, to inculcate the necessity of great and nice attention to every part of dress, as well to what was hid as to what was seen. (I knew she wore coarse petticoats, coarse shifts and thread stockings and these never well washed or changed enough.) I observed that a long toilette was necessary and gave her no credit for boasting that hers was a short one.'

Malmesbury accompanied Caroline to England and introduced her to the Prince on April 5, 1795. 'I according to the established etiquette introduced (no one else being in the room) the Princess Caroline to him. She very properly, in consequence of my saying it was the right mode of proceeding, attempted to kneel to him. He raised her gracefully enough and embraced her, said barely one word, turned round, retired to a distant part of the apartment and, calling to me, said: "Harris, I am not well: pray get me a glass of brandy." I said: "Sir, had you not better have a glass of water?" Upon which he, much out of humour, said *with an oath*: "No, I will go directly to the Queen." And away he went.'

Caroline, bewildered by George's strange behaviour asked: 'Mon Dieu! Is he always like that? I find him very fat and not at all like the picture sent me.'

Three days later, the marriage took place with customary state. It was performed at night and the Archbishop of Canterbury officiated. In the morning, the Prince of Wales had driven down to Mrs Fitzherbert's house at Twickenham. Immediately before the wedding, the Royal family dined at Buckingham House and, as they went to dress for the ceremony the King instructed his second son, the Duke of Clarence (the future William IV) to go with the Prince of Wales and not to leave him because of the state of depression that he was in. Clarence recorded that the Prince never uttered a word until they were on their way back to St James's Palace when he suddenly said: 'William, I wish you to go to Mrs Fitzherbert tomorrow and tell her I assure her she is the only woman I have ever loved.'

During the wedding itself the Prince, who seemed dazed, rose impatiently from his knees before the ceremony was half over. The Archbishop stopped, but the King stepped forward and recalled his son to his situation. At the end of the service he 'shook his son's hand with a force that brought tears to his eyes.' It is improbable, considering what had gone before, that

George's 'daze' was due to drink any more than his tears were the result of a septuagenarian handshake. But once the marriage was a fact, he certainly got as drunk as he could and spent most of his wedding night in the grate 'where he fell' said Caroline 'and where I left him.'

Charlotte, the child of George and Caroline, was born on January 7, 1796; on January 10, George made the passionate will in favour of Mrs Fitzherbert. He then openly left Caroline and eventually, in response to her complaints and enquiries, wrote to her on April 30: 'Madam, as Lord Cholmondeley informs me that you wish I would define in writing the terms upon which we are to live, I shall endeavour to explain myself on that head with as much clearness and with as much propriety as the nature of the subject will admit. Our inclinations are not in our power, nor should either of us be held answerable to the other because nature has not made us suitable to each other. Tranquil and comfortable society is, however, in our power; let our intercourse, therefore, be restricted to that and I will distinctly subscribe the condition which you required through Lady Cholmondeley that, even in the event of any accident happening to my daughter (which I trust Providence in its mercy will avert) I shall not infringe the terms of the restriction by proposing, at any period, a connection of a more particular nature. I shall now finally close this disagreeable correspondence, trusting that, as we have completely explained ourselves to each other, the rest of our lives will be passed in uninterrupted tranquillity. I am, Madam, with great truth, very sincerely yours, George P.'

Caroline replied in a letter beginning: 'The avowal of your conversation with Lord Cholmondeley neither surprises nor offends me; it merely confirmed *what you have tacitly insinuated for this twelvemonth.*' She retired to a villa at Charlton, which had once been occupied by Mrs Fitzherbert. In 1801, she removed to Montague House, Blackheath and here she continued to receive many visitors, including some from abroad who took advantage of the Peace of Amiens to visit England. At the end of 1802 she adopted, as a newly-born baby, William Austin.

That Caroline had what can only be described as a craze for children is undoubted. It was of such dimensions as to be something more positive than what is loosely described as a 'thwarted maternal interest.' In her later years, the parents of any child to whom she took a fancy were destined for promotion. Her interest in 'petite Victorine,' the daughter of Bartolomeo Bergami, was to be the cause of her advancement of the father, which provided a lasting scandal and led to her trial. At the end of her life, the attraction of the little son of Parson Wood which she 'could not control' and which, according to Brougham, 'amounted almost to a craze,' caused her to dismiss her faithful friends Lord and Lady Hood as Lord of the Bedchamber and Mistress of the Robes 'in order to appoint Wood and his wife who had not the proper rank and indeed in all respects were unfit for the situation.' And in these early days at Blackheath there was a veritable nursery.

In his *Travels in England in the year* 1803, a French visitor, J. H. Compé, encouraged by Caroline, described her life at Blackheath with 'eight or nine poor orphan children to whom she had the condescension to supply the place of mother.' The author draws a picture which bears the stamp of Caroline's approval and was later incorporated into the official defence of her character. 'These poor children were boarded by her with honest people in the neighbourhood; she not only directed everything relative to their education and instruction but sent every day to converse with them and thus contributed to the formation of their infant minds. Never while I live shall I forget the charming, the affecting scene which I had the happiness of witnessing when the Princess was pleased to introduce me to her little foster-children . . .

'The children appeared clothed in the cleanest, but at the same time in the simplest, manner just as the children of country people are in general dressed. They seemed perfectly ignorant of the high rank of their foster-mother, or rather not to comprehend it. The sight of a stranger somewhat abashed them; but their bashfulness soon wore off and they appeared to be perfectly at home. Their dignified benefactress conversed with them in a lively, jocose and truly maternal manner. She called to her first one, then another, and another and, among the rest a little boy, five or six years old, who had a sore upon his face. Many a parent of too delicate nerves would not have been able to look at her own child in this state without an unpleasant sensation. Not so the royal mother of these orphans. She called the boy to her, gave him a biscuit, looked at his face to see whether it had got any better and manifested no repugnance when the grateful infant pressed her hand to his bosom.

'What this wise, royal instructress said to me on this occasion is too deeply impressed upon my memory to be erased. "People find fault with me," she said, "for not doing more for these children, even after I have taken them under my care. I ought, in their opinion, to provide them with more elegant and costly clothes, to keep masters of every kind for them that they may make a figure as persons of refined education. However, I laugh at their censure, for I know what I am about. It is not my intention to raise these children into a rank superior to that in which they are placed: in that rank I mean them to remain and to become useful, virtuous and happy members of society. The boys are destined to become expert seamen and the girls skilful, sensible, industrious housewives—nothing more——"

'Such was the wise and philanthropic manner in which this admirable Princess, in the flower of her age, passed one day after another. . . . She devoted one day in the week to her own daughter, the Princess Charlotte, who came to see her and spent the day with her. There was nothing to prevent her from enjoying this gratification oftener, for the child was to be brought to her whenever she pleased. For wise reasons, however, she denied herself and her daughter the more frequent repetition of a pleasure of which both of them every day were ardently desirous. "If," she said, "I were to have the child with me every day, I should be obliged sometimes to speak to her in a tone of displeasure and even of severity. She would then have less affection for me and what I said would make less impression upon her heart." '

What M. Compé omitted to notice was that William Austin, the child of a sail-maker from Deptford, was inseparable from his foster-mother and brought up not at all according to his station. And what posterity has noticed is that, making all allowance for the thirty-five-year-old Caroline's undoubted interest in other people's children, this kind of establishment was the perfect way of concealing any personal experiments in maternity she might be inclined to make.

Meanwhile 'Willikin' became only too well known to many illustrious visitors, including Mr Pitt. 'Oh! how Mr Pitt used to frown' recorded Lady Hester Stanhope, 'when he was brought in after dinner and held up by a footman to take up anything out of the dessert he liked, bawling and kicking down the wine and hung up by his breeches over the table for people to laugh at . . . the Princess used to say to Mr Pitt: "Don't you think he is a nice boy?" To which Pitt would reply: "I don't understand anything about children." Once he cried for a spider on the ceiling and, though they gave him all sorts of playthings to divert his attention, he would have nothing but the spider. Then there was such a calling of footmen and long sticks and such a to-do!'

Caroline's most intimate friends at this period were Sir John and Lady Douglas, her neighbours at Blackheath. At the end of 1804, Lady Douglas was suddenly dismissed from intimacy, found herself the recipient of unpleasant letters and drawings and ultimately retaliated by making the charges against Caroline which led Augustus, Duke of Sussex, in the November of 1805 to wait on his brother, George, Prince of Wales, with news which 'might affect the royal succession.' The so-called 'Delicate Investigation' was thereupon by order of the King undertaken by Lords Erskine, Grenville, Spencer and Ellenborough whom in the July of 1806 furnished a report acquitting Caroline of being the mother of William Austin, but adding that 'as on the one hand the facts of pregnancy and delivery are to our minds satisfactorily disproved, so on the other hand we think that . . . circumstances . . . particularly those stated to have

43

passed between Her Royal Highness and Captain Manby must be credited until they shall receive some decisive contradiction, and, if true, are justly entitled to the most serious consideration.'

The former Chancellor Lord Eldon; Spencer Perceval, the former Attorney-General; the Solicitor-General, Sir Vicary Gibbs, and others leapt to Caroline's defence. (Perceval even gave tongue to the sentiment: 'To the Tower or the scaffold in such a Cause'—which makes Caroline's later admission to Brougham that 'she had humbugged Perceval, Eldon and the whole lot' sound rather shabby.) Under their expert legal advice and tuition, she made a masterly defence of herself in letters to the King and was eventually received at Court once more. But, in the years that followed, the matter intruded into politics and finally into the popular consciousness. The Government were asked why Lady Douglas had not been prosecuted for perjury and could be given no answer other than that there were reasons which made it inadvisable. It was to the general relief of everyone concerned that in 1813 Caroline asked and was by Parliament granted permission to reside abroad and in the summer of 1814, accompanied by her attendants and 'young Mr Austin,' set out, under the name of the Countess of Wolfenbüttel on her fantastic odyssey.

[iv] William Austin

On Christmas Day, 1814, George, in the presence of his sister, Mary, had a serious conversation with his daughter Charlotte about William Austin. He told her: 'As long as I am alive this boy can be of no sort of consequence, but that if I should die then the boy may be a very serious misfortune to you as well as to the country.' For years both the Prince Regent and the King had prohibited Charlotte, on her visits to her mother, ever seeing William Austin, because 'from two points of view he was an improper companion' for her.

Charlotte told her father that 'she had never seen him in the drawing-room from the time the order was given that she was not to keep company with him' but that as her mother greatly preferred him to her and always had him with her in whichever of her houses she was in, it was impossible altogether to avoid meeting him. She had in fact met him on the staircase, 'a sickly-looking child with fair hair and blue eyes.'

Her father's theories impressed Charlotte. When she discussed the matter with her aunt Mary, she said: 'Now I see clearly that my mother's object is to bring this boy forward.'

'But as long as your father is alive,' said Princess Mary, 'he can be of no consequence.'

To which Charlotte surprisingly answered: 'So my father thinks, but I am not so sure of that.'

'But,' said Princess Mary, 'I believe the Prince can prove that he has not been for *many* years under the same roof with the Princess.'

'The Princess of Wales,' replied Charlotte, 'has been at Carlton House since she had Blackheath and, though I was very young, I am sure I remember seeing Captain Manby and Miss Manby his sister at Carlton House.'

Towards the end of February, George wrote to his daughter, who had now had two months to see the situation in perspective: 'You are now completely sensible and satisfied that she has interests, attachments

45

and views which must render it the object of her most anxious wish and endeavour to prejudice you in the opinion of the whole world and if possible, however unnatural it should seem, to ruin you for the benefit of another. That the time may come when she will thus exert her utmost efforts in favour of the boy . . . there can be no doubt. In such a sad predicament, when I am gone you have no protector but a husband; and that husband cannot be a protector unless he shall have a name, a station and a character in Europe calculated to repel what may be, and what you and I now do clearly see will be, attempted.'

It seems to me, from this, to be quite clear that whatever they might officially pretend and however publicly (and even thankfully) they might accept the finding of the 'Delicate Investigation' that William Austin was the son of Sophia Austin, the entire Royal Family was satisfied that Caroline was the mother of the boy and that the father, though possibly Captain Manby, must be presumed to be George because Caroline had been careful, at the critical time, to spend the night under the same roof with him at Carlton House. In other words, Caroline could, if she wanted, establish William Austin as the heir-male to the Throne.

Caroline's answer at the time, when someone accused her of being the boy's mother: 'Prove it—and he shall be your King' was not, therefore, as it has usually been interpreted, a laughing assertion of her innocence, a light dismissal of a monstrous *canard* against a faithful wife. It was an equivocal, double-edged remark and the edge turned against the Royal Family was the sharp and cutting reminder that if they allowed the 'Delicate Investigation' to establish her maternity, it would also establish William Austin, as George's presumed child, as the future Sovereign.

It is also noteworthy that Princess Charlotte's remark about her mother being at Carlton House (which it was altogether against her interest to admit) corroborates the vital evidence, ten years earlier, of Lady Douglas (which the 'Delicate Investigation' dismissed as untrue) that when Caroline had told her of her pregnancy, though she would not reveal who was the father, she did say that she hoped it would be a boy and that 'if it was discovered she would give the Prince of Wales the credit of being the father, for she had slept two nights at Carlton House within the year.'

These facts are an essential clue to the meaning of the 'Delicate Investigation.' All historians and biographers, as far as I know, have made the situation appear simpler than it was. They have assumed that George wished to prove Caroline guilty in order to have an opportunity of divorcing her. But in fact, as is now obvious enough, it was far more important to George than it was to Caroline to establish that she was innocent, even though no one, least of all George himself, believed it.

Lord Glenbervie, Lord North's son-in-law, who was a lawyer, a scholar, a Privy Councillor, a lord of the treasury—an observer both responsible and knowledgeable—records in his diary how, during a visit to Caroline, ' "Little Willy" as the Princess calls him, concerning whose parents the enquiry was during the *Delicate Investigation*, was in the room after dinner as, it seems, is usual on such occasions, and was playing with an orange which Lady Glenbervie had given him when the Princess, in a sort of reverie, after looking at him steadfastly, said, in her imperfect English, "It is a long time since I brought you to bed, Willy." The boy not hearing distinctly showed that he did not by some gesture or expression, on which she said again, "It is a long time now since I brought you to bed." Still not understanding what was meant, he seemed to have thought she had said it was a long time since he ought to have gone to bed, for he replied that he would go to bed immediately and went out of the room. Lady Glenbervie, prepared as she is for many strange things, was astonished and confounded beyond measure. This is a secret that must be at least a century old before it ought to be whispered, and I give my son that solemn caution if ever this part of this journal shall fall under his eyes.'*

Glenbervie also recorded the relationship of Caroline and Prince Louis Ferdinand: 'Prince Lewis of Prussia, nephew to the old Princess of Orange and to the late King of Prussia, was *l'amant de coeur* of the Princess of Wales and had *les prémices de son coeur* long before she came to England. There is reason to believe he came to England *incognito* after her marriage and when she was living at Charlton and saw her in private and those who have the best means for guessing believe little Edwardina, a protegée of Her Royal Highness, was the result. Willie is thought to be the offspring either of Captain Manby or of Sir Sidney Smith.'†

* This part of the diary was not published till 1928. Considerable portions of it are still unpublished.

† Princess Charlotte, on the other hand, said she thought that Edwardina was Sir Sydney Smith's child and that she was certain that Willie was Captain Manby's. It seems more probable that both children were Prince Louis's, who, it will be remembered, Mrs Fitzherbert had reason to suppose was Caroline's real husband, just as she was George's real wife.

Caroline's own account of William Austin's parentage was given in the March of 1819 under the seal of secrecy to James Brougham, the brother of her lawyer, Henry Brougham, who was to defend her at her trial. The only person to whom James was allowed to reveal it was to Henry, under the same seal of secrecy.

'She began by saying,' recorded James Brougham, 'she had "humbugged Perceval, Eldon and the whole lot" and that William was not the son of Austin; that he was the natural son of Prince Louis Ferdinand and was brought over to England in 1803 by a German woman who died about five years ago; that Louis Ferdinand sent him to her to take care of. On his arrival (she expected him) she got a child from Austin, which accidentally had a mark on its arm the same as William; that this child was taken God knows where, but sent away, and that William was substituted in his place; that she contrived so that the mother did not see it for some time and she never knew or suspected that it had been changed and of course believes to this hour that William is her son.

'In 1805 or 1806 Louis Ferdinand came over to see the Princess. Captain Manby, who had been introduced to her by Lady Townsend, was on that station and was entrusted to bring him over. She saw him as often as she could during the week he was here.

'She was always attached to Louis Ferdinand and said she could never love the Prince as her heart was engaged to Louis Ferdinand, but had he treated her well she would have respected him and been a good wife, though there could be no love. Says she made a fool of Manby. . .

'Louis Ferdinand was nephew to Frederick the Great and was killed at Jena. She says he courted death and

49

insinuated that he was in love with her all his life. . .

'After she told me, she said her mind was easier at having told someone of this and frequently afterwards asked me if I thought William looked like a carpenter's son—and whether he did not betray his blood by looking so like a German and things of that sort.'

But it seems that James Brougham was not the only recipient of this confidence. Years after everyone concerned was dead, Henry Brougham placed it on record about 'the sailmaker's child at Deptford, who was called Billy Austin, but for whom another was substituted after a few years, the child of one of her ladies in Germany by Prince Louis of Prussia,' that 'she had often mentioned this to Lady Charlotte Lindsay and Mrs Damer, but they supposed it was a jest. However, when Lushington and Wilde went with the funeral to Germany and one of them presented the other to the general who came to receive the body and then said: "And here is Mr Austin, of whom you have often heard," he said, "Yes, I have often heard of Billy Austin, but this is not he; this is the son of my old general, Prince William,* and so like him that I at once knew him before you named him." '

In assessing the truth of Caroline's story that, though Louis Ferdinand was the father, she was not the mother, it must be borne in mind that the one man above all to whom she could not admit her maternity (if it were true) was Henry Brougham. He had to defend her against the charges which were being prepared for her trial and the whole basis of his case was her complete

* Louis Ferdinand had both an uncle and a cousin who might be this 'Prince William' who is unidentifiable.

innocence. Psychologically she had to believe that he believed it and it is unlikely that she ever noticed—as the wits did—that in his subsequent declaration that 'the Queen is pure innocence' the last word sounded like 'in a sense.'

Secondly, if Captain Manby was in the secret, it would explain as nothing else can, Caroline's public indiscretions, 'making a fool of him.' To shield Louis Ferdinand, any ruse was permissible; and one must read the following entry in Glenbervie's diaries with this in mind: 'I can never forget my astonishment when on going to dine at Blackheath some time before the "Delicate Investigation" I found Captain Manby there . . . He was certainly not, from his situation, birth or manners, a person one would expect to meet in the society of the Princess of Wales. We were only five: Her Royal Highness, Lady Glenbervie, Miss Vernon, myself and the Captain. She placed him next her at table and directed all her *looks*, words and *attentions* to him at and after dinner, when we went to coffee and then she made him sit very close to her on the same sofa. After a time he withdrew and the moment he shut the door she started up and said in her broken English, "Child cry" and then hurried into the adjoining room which has a communication with her garden and park. She has a private key to this which she sometimes lends. She was absent from us perhaps three-quarters of an hour and to do her justice she returned with an air and look of confusion. In about ten minutes we took our leave, having to return to Town that night. I never saw Manby with her but that time. The child was little Billy.'

It need only be added that by the date this occasion could easily have coincided with Prince Louis

Ferdinand's visit to England under Captain Manby's escort and that it is thus not beyond the bounds of possibility that the private invitation to the Glenbervies was part of a deliberate plan on Caroline's part.

Thirdly, Caroline always treated William Austin as if he were her own child. As long as she lived, he was never parted from her. On March 5, 1818 she wrote to her bankers, Messrs Coutts, instructing them to invest £200 a year (the rental of her house at Blackheath) in Government stock on William Austin's behalf. On her death in 1821, she left him all her property and though her estate was insolvent, he received £4,000 from the executors.

He spent most of the rest of his life abroad where, (since he had left England with Caroline when he was ten and had only returned for the unhappy months that saw Caroline's trial, her exclusion from the Coronation and her death), he was more at home than in the country of his birth. He was certified insane by Italian doctors in the autumn of 1841, which by an odd coincidence was the time that Queen Victoria gave birth to the future Edward VII. He was kept in an asylum in Milan until 1845 when he was taken to England and immured in Dr Sutherland's private asylum in Chelsea till his death four years later.

One may say, therefore, that there is a considerable probability that William Austin was the son of Caroline at a time when George could have been presumed the father and that the boy was therefore legally heir to the Throne. That, in the chestful of documents removed from the Public Record Office in 1935, the proof of this lay is a possibility which is supported by the fact that the remaining folder HO 126/3 does not

THE WIVES OF KING GEORGE IV

contain many of the documents which it is said to contain.

The documents listed as being there but in fact abstracted from it include a letter from Caroline to the King, December 8, 1806: the Lord Chancellor to the King, November 27, 1806: the King to the Lord Chancellor, November 29, 1806 and December 11, 1806: the minutes of the Cabinets of December 23, 1806 and January 25, 1807: Lord Chancellor to the King with enclosure from Lord Ellenborough: a letter from Caroline to the King, February 16, 1807: Prince of Wales to the King and opinion of H.R.H.'s Law Officers annexed February 28, 1807: the King to the Lord Chancellor, March 3, 1807: the Lord Chancellor to the King on the same date and again on March 11: Minute of the Cabinet of March 20, 1807, and a separate Minute annexed from the Chancellor, March 25—all of which obviously relate to the 'Delicate Investigation.'

The status of William Austin is of mere academic interest today. Even if he were, and could be proved to have been, the titular Prince of Wales, it would only mean that he, and not the Duke of Clarence, should on George IV's death have been King William IV and that Queen Victoria should not have succeeded to the Throne until 1849, instead of, as she did, in 1837. She was, in any case, the eventual heiress.

But, when Caroline left England, with William Austin safely in her possession, in 1814, the matter was anything but academic. And it is this which explains the subsequent events which were to culminate in Caroline's trial. The Crown had two explosive secrets. One was the fact that the Prince Regent's true wife was Maria

Fitzherbert, which, had it been known, would have meant that George would immediately have had to renounce the Succession under the Act of Settlement. The other was the existence of William Austin who, if Caroline cared to proclaim and prove him her son, could complicate the succession even more hopelessly. George, in fact, could be blackmailed by both his wives. Though there was no danger of it from Maria Fitzherbert, Caroline of Brunswick was incalculable.

Thus, for the remaining seven years of Caroline's life, George's one desire was to discredit and, if possible, divorce her. To attain this end, there was nothing that he would stop at and, when the trial is put in perspective, the reader may be disposed to think that there is very little that he did.

[v] Prelude to the Trial

Caroline, after making various visits, determined to settle in Italy where she eventually bought the Villa d'Este on the shore of Lake Como. As most of her English attendants, outraged by her eccentric conduct at Courts she called at, left her, she collected a household of Italians of whom the most notable was Bartolomeo Bergami, a six-foot military man with 'large mustachios and whiskers, dark complexion and eyes, a bold but agreeable countenance and of robust form,' to whose small daughter, Victorine, she had taken a violent fancy. She made him her Chamberlain.

'As to my household,' she said, 'all de fine English folk leave me. I know people are very ill-natured and choose to abuse me. No matter, I do not care—from henceforth I will do just as I please, that I will. Since de English do not give me the great honour of being Princess of Wales, I will be Caroline—a happy, merry soul.' In her merriment, she sang duets with Napoleon's wife, the Empress Marie Louise, at Berne; gave a grand party to Murat in Naples, where she appeared as Glory and 'even more ridiculously dressed than the others, tripped forward, took a feather from the wing of Renown and wrote in large golden letters on a panel she held the names of the different battles in which Murat had distinguished himself'; and organized a *fête champêtre* at the Villa d'Este where she exhibited herself as a Druidical priestess with Willikins as the sacrificial victim. She then decided to spend the next year, 1816, in making an expedition to the East.

Her impending absence suited George. At the end of 1815, the marriage was arranged between the Princess Charlotte and Prince Leopold of Saxe-Coburg-Saalfeld and, with the prospect of the succession now being safeguarded, it had become more imperative than ever to rid himself of the menace of Caroline. In the January of 1816, Castlereagh, the Foreign Secretary, acting on George's instructions wrote a 'Most Private and Secret' letter (which fortunately has survived) to his brother in Italy to instruct him that any evidence which might be to Caroline's discredit was to be scrupulously collected.

'You will keep in mind,' the letter ran, 'that there are two objects to be aimed at. The first and best would be unqualified proofs of what no person could morally doubt as would for ever deliver the Prince Regent from the scandal of having a woman so lost to all decency in

55

the relation of his wife—to effect this, or to justify in
prudence a proceeding for Divorce, the proofs must be
direct and unequivocal and the evidence such with
respect to the parties to be examined as would preclude
their testimony from being run down and discredited.
. . . But there is another most important object short of
Divorce viz., to accumulate such a body of evidence as
may at any time enable the Prince Regent to justify
himself for refusing to receive the Princess in this
country or to admit her to the enjoyment of any of
those honorary distinctions to which his wife, if received
into his Court and family, would be entitled.'

In February, 1816, Prince Leopold arrived in England
formally to ask for Charlotte's hand: in the March of
1816, Castlereagh's brother was able to report that, in
Italy, everything was in train in Caroline's absence and
that he had 'written to the gardener's boy and the cook
at the Villa d'Este and they are expected here to finish
the Carnival when we shall see if there is anything to be
done with them': on May 2, 1816, in London, Charlotte
and Leopold were married: and at the beginning of
September, 1816, Guiseppe Rastelli, who was to give
the crucial evidence against Caroline, successfully
applied to her immediately on her return from her
journeyings for the post of her Superintendent of Stables
at the Villa d'Este.

These dates are necessary for understanding the true
course of events, because the official version (which was
the only one known at the time and which is still
repeated by historians apparently ignorant of Castlereagh's 'Most Private and Secret' letter) was that it
was not until over a year later, in 1817, after the death
of Princess Charlotte in child-birth, that George started

to investigate Caroline's conduct. And as Rastelli left Caroline's service in 1817, months before the setting up of the Milan Commission which considered the evidence collected against her, it is assumed that he was, even if a rascal and a perjurer, at least a relatively impartial witness. Once the real sequence of events is seen, it is quite obvious that he was 'planted' at the Villa d'Este by George's agents. And even in assuming that he was engaged by Caroline immediately on her return, I am giving him the benefit of a doubt. He said in his evidence that he entered her service 'at the latter end of August or the beginning of September, 1816' and that she was, at that time, in residence at the Villa d'Este. No reliance can really be placed on his word, but it is worth noticing that, if the August date were the true one, he would have been introduced into her household on the eve of her return.

The public proceedings against Caroline were not long delayed. Princess Charlotte died in the November of 1817, when Caroline was, in the course of further journeyings, visiting Warsaw. Prompted, so it was averred, by the reports to the Admiralty of Captain Pechell, who had been in command of the frigate *Clorinde* which had taken Caroline to the East, and by the gossip of some of Caroline's servants which the Duke of Cumberland had heard in Brussels, enquiries were set on foot. Immediately after Charlotte's death, George instructed his creature, Leach, to ask for a commission to be set up to investigate Caroline's conduct. The ministry agreed and the tribunal assembled in Milan in the September of 1818. From time to time it sent copies of the evidence collected to Leach who passed it on to the Prime Minister. A prominent member of the

Commission was Lord Stewart the brother of Castlereagh who had received the secret instructions at the
beginning of 1816 and the courier and carrier of Lord
Stewart's private messages to Westphalia and Frankfort,
to Paris and Vienna, scouring Europe for witnesses, was
Guiseppe Rastelli.

The Commission returned to England and made its
report in the July of 1819. When George's ministers
(including Castlereagh) had studied it, they felt bound
to advise the Prince Regent in these terms: 'According
to these opinions Your Royal Highness's servants are
led to believe that the facts stated in the papers which
have been referred to them would furnish sufficient proof
of the crime, provided they were established by credible
witnesses; but it is at the same time the opinion of Your
Royal Highness's confidential servants that, considering
the manner in which a great part of this testimony has
unavoidably been obtained, and the circumstances that
the persons who have afforded it are foreigners, many
of whom appear to be in a low station of life, it would
not be possible to advise Your Royal Highness to
institute any legal proceedings upon such evidence,
without further enquiry as to the characters and
circumstances of the witnesses by whom it is to be
supported.'

As a comment of this important memorandum, one
can only endorse Fitzgerald's remark that it is 'as
damaging a piece of evidence against the Regent's
ministers as could be conceived; for here was the
deliberate opinion as to the value of the evidence on
which they later brought the Queen to trial.' Fitzgerald
thought that it showed 'how flexible were their principles'; a truer estimate which we may make, having at

our disposal more facts of the case than he had, is that it showed how imperative it was for George, at whatever risk, to discredit Caroline.

The death of the old, mad King, at the end of January, 1820—six months after this Cabinet advice—and the accession of the Prince Regent as George IV made the matter even more urgent. Caroline, though by now aware of the extent of the plot against her, determined to come to England and assert her rights as Queen. Neither the obstacles that were put in her way—such as a refusal of a *visa*—nor the offer of £50,000 a year if she would remain on the Continent, had any effect. In February, George threatened to dismiss his Ministers and retire to Hanover unless the Government instituted proceedings against the Queen. Again they replied that they were in duty bound to advise him that 'the body of testimony consists almost exclusively of the evidence of foreigners, most of them not above the rank of menial servants, or that of waiters and attendants in hotels, wholly unacquainted with the English language and some of the former class standing in the questionable situation of having been dismissed or removed from Her Royal Highness's service.'

On the other hand, they agreed that Caroline's name was to be omitted from the Prayer Book.

Caroline, when she heard of it, immediately wrote to know why and, intimating that she intended to be crowned Queen, started her return journey to England. At the beginning of June she landed at Dover where she was unexpectedly (owing to a failure of Government staff-work) greeted with a Royal Salute from the Castle. The whole town lined the shore and she was given the first of those hysterical popular ovations which were to become a feature of English life for the next five months and bring the country to the brink of revolution.

On June 6, London saw her for the first time for seven years. She was dressed for the occasion in a black twilled sarcenet gown, a fur tippet and a ruff, with a hat of black satin and feathers. She was now fifty-two, stout and matronly, and neither her ringlets nor the roses on her cheeks were her own. But her tears of emotion were. She had not dared to hope for such a welcome. The streets were almost impassable. Every window was filled with eager faces and men and women waving white handkerchiefs. Cries of 'Long Live Queen Caroline' mingled with 'God bless her. She has a noble spirit. She must be innocent.' To give point to their sentiments, the crowd smashed Lady Hertford's windows in Manchester Square.

Though Caroline's cavalcade had not intended to take the Pall Mall route to South Audley Street where she was staying temporarily in the house of one of her principal supporters, Alderman Wood, the pressure of people and the cries of 'To Carlton House!' forced it. The sentries presented arms and Caroline waved her handkerchief and called 'God save the King' as she passed.

Meanwhile, earlier that same day, George had declared open war. He had sent this message to the House of Lords, commending his Queen to be dealt with by them—the first instance of the kind since the precedent of King Henry VIII:

'The King thinks it necessary, in consequence of the arrival of the Queen, to communicate to the House of Lords certain papers respecting the conduct of Her Majesty since her departure from this kingdom, which he recommends to the immediate and serious attention of this House.

'The King has felt the most anxious desire to avert the necessity of disclosures and discussions which must be as painful to his people as they can be to himself; but the step now taken by the Queen leaves him no alternative.

'The King has the fullest confidence that, in consequence of this communication, the House of Lords will adopt that course of proceeding which the justice of the case and the honour and dignity of His Majesty's crown may require.'

The papers were deposited on the table of the House in two large green brief bags. From this moment 'green bag' meaning 'tainted evidence' became one of the catchwords of the nation.

Princess Lieven wrote to Metternich: 'We live in continual tumult and anxiety. The Queen will age us all. Troops have been brought up round London and, at night, cavalry pickets occupy the principal quarters of the town.' Later, she added, 'The Queen is greeted with respect and enthusiasm not only by the mob— make no mistake about that—but by the solid middle-classes who have won England her reputation for virtue and morality. The streets are full of well-dressed men and respectable women, all waving their hats and their handkerchiefs. In a few days there will be a serious crisis in the country. The Queen's trial begins next week.'

The method of proceeding against Caroline eventually chosen was by a 'Bill to deprive Her Majesty Caroline Amelia Elizabeth of the Title, Prerogatives, Privileges and Pretensions of Queen Consort of this realm and to dissolve the marriage between His Majesty and the said Queen.' The Bill stated that 'whereas in the year 1814 Her Majesty, being in Milan in Italy, engaged in her service in a menial situation one Bartolomeo Bergami, a foreigner of low station; and whereas, after the said Bartolomeo Bergami had so entered the service of Her Royal Highness, a most unbecoming intimacy commenced between them and Her Royal Highness not only advanced the said Bartolomeo Bergami to a high situation in Her Royal Highness's household but bestowed on him other great and extraordinary marks of favour and distinction, obtained for him orders of knighthood and titles of honour and conferred upon him a pretended order of knighthood which Her Royal Highness had taken upon herself to institute without any just or lawful authority; and whereas her said Royal Highness, while the said Bartolomeo Bergami was in her said service, unmindful of her exalted rank and station and of her duty to Your Majesty and wholly regardless of her own honour and character, conducted herself towards the said Bartolomeo Bergami, both in public and private, in the various places and countries which Her Royal Highness visited, with indecent and offensive familiarity and freedom, and carried on a licentious, disgraceful and adulterous intercourse with the said Bartolomeo Bergami, which continued for a long period of time during Her Royal Highness's residence abroad, by which conduct of her said Royal Highness great scandal and dishonour have been brought upon Your Majesty's family and this Kingdom:

'Therefore, to manifest our deep sense of such scandalous, disgraceful and vicious conduct on the part of her said Majesty, by which she has violated the duty she owed to Your Majesty and has rendered herself unworthy of the exalted rank and station of Queen Consort of this realm, and to evince our just regard for the dignity of the crown and the honour of this nation, we, Your Majesty's most dutiful and loyal subjects, the Lords Spiritual and Temporal and Commons in Parliament assembled, do hereby entreat Your Majesty that it may be enacted:

'And be it enacted by the King's most excellent Majesty, by and with the advice and consent of the Lords Spiritual and Temporal and Commons in this present Parliament assembled, and by the authority of the same, that her said Majesty Caroline Amelia Elizabeth, from and after the passing of this Act, shall be and is hereby deprived of the title of Queen, and of all prerogatives, rights, privileges and exemptions appertaining to her as Queen Consort of this realm; and that her said Majesty shall, from and after the passing of this Act, for ever be disabled and rendered incapable of using, exercising and enjoying the same or any of them; and moreover that the marriage between His Majesty and the said Caroline Amelia Elizabeth be, and the same is hereby from henceforth, for ever wholly dissolved, annulled and made void to all intents, constructions and purposes whatsoever.'

The day appointed for the opening of the debate on the Bill (the proceeding popularly known in history by its less exact if truer description, 'the trial of Queen Caroline') was August 19, 1820. For the previous three days London had been in a ferment. Westminster was a network of barricades with bodies of those soldiers who could still be trusted not to mutiny at every corner. As the Queen, on the way to the House, passed Carlton House, the crowds watched with feverish anxiety to see whether the guards would present arms. When they did so, men surged forward to shake hands with them and women to kiss them. Cries were heard thunderously: 'The Queen or Death' and 'We'll give our blood for you.' On walls were chalked 'The Queen for ever: the King in the river.' Beams a foot square which had been thrown across the streets were broken as if they had been reeds by the mere pressure of the multitude. The crowd outside Westminster was estimated at between twenty and thirty thousand. The King did not dare show himself. Castlereagh, though willing to, was officially prevented lest he should be lynched and had a bed installed in the Foreign Office in the room in which he gave audience to foreign ambassadors.

The House of Lords was crowded. There was a fine of 500 guineas a day for non-attendance unless age, infirmity, absence abroad or the Roman Catholic faith provided a valid excuse.

Caroline, cheered to the echo outside, took her place in silence inside on the crimson and gilt chair facing the Throne which had been provided for her. She wore a black figured gauze dress, trimmed with much lace, a high ruff, white sleeves and a white veil. Though she had by nature light hair, blue eyes, a fair complexion and a good-humoured expression, she had by artifice spoilt her appearance with much rouge, a black wig and a profusion of false curls, which 'gave her features an air of boldness and defiance.' It was Caroline's misfortune that she always managed to dress, act and speak in a part which was not herself and to do all of them badly. She was a figure of simplicity and tragedy. She appeared a rather shady figure of fun.

The witnesses, a motley crew from the Italian underworld whose depositions the Green Bag contained, were living in a state of seige in the houses of the officers of the House of Lords. Walls had been hastily built to prevent them being seen as they took exercise and they were guarded by a gun-boat patrolling the Thames and a regiment of soldiers on the land side. Nevertheless, as Lord Albemarle put it, 'about the building in which they were immured from August until September, the London mob hovered like a cat round the cage of a canary.'

Caroline's reaction to the first witness, Theodore Majocchi who had been her postilion, was unfortunate. When he came forward Caroline 'stood up close to him and threw her veil completely back, held her body very backward and placed both her arms at her sides. In this position she stared furiously at him. For some seconds there was dead silence. Then she screamed out "Theodore!" in a most frantic manner and rushed violently out of the House.'

People were divided in opinion as to what this exhibition meant. Some, forgetting that the Queen knew he would be there, considered it a proof of her guilt. Others, more reasonably, construed it as an indignant protest at 'seeing her servant dressed up and turned into a gentleman' as well as at his ingratitude. The

Prime Minister immediately sent a messenger to inform the King, who considered the 'O, Theodore!' a fact of greatest importance.

But whatever advantage George might have hoped to gain from it was speedily dispelled by Majocchi's cross-examination by Brougham in the course of which he provided London with a new catchword: 'Non mi ricordo'—'I don't remember.'

A mere sample must serve as illustration of what was a long process:

ATTORNEY-GENERAL: At what time did you meet with Bergami at Naples?

MAJOCCHI: About Christmas 1814.

ATTORNEY-GENERAL: In what situation was he at the time?

MAJOCCHI: He was a courier—and, it was reported, equerry.

ATTORNEY-GENERAL: Did you afterward enter the service of the Princess?

MAJOCCHI: I did.

ATTORNEY-GENERAL: How long after you had met with Bergami?

MAJOCCHI: About a fortnight.

ATTORNEY-GENERAL: What was then the situation of Bergami?

MAJOCCHI: He was a lackey and wore a livery.

ATTORNEY-GENERAL: Can you recollect any accident happening to Bergami?

MAJOCCHI: Yes.

ATTORNEY-GENERAL: What was it and where did it happen?

MAJOCCHI: A kick from a horse. When they went to the lake Aniano.

ATTORNEY-GENERAL: In consequence of it, was he put to bed?

MAJOCCHI: Yes.

ATTORNEY-GENERAL: Did you see the Princess in his room during his sickness?

MAJOCCHI: Yes.

ATTORNEY-GENERAL: Did you carry broth to him?

MAJOCCHI: Yes, often.

ATTORNEY-GENERAL: Did you see the Princess on that occasion?

MAJOCCHI: Non mi ricordo—I don't remember.

ATTORNEY-GENERAL: Were any instructions given to you as to where to sleep after this accident?

MAJOCCHI: Yes, I slept on a sofa in the cabinet.

ATTORNEY-GENERAL: Did you see anyone pass during those nights through the corridor?

MAJOCCHI: Yes, I did. Her Royal Highness.

ATTORNEY-GENERAL: In what manner?

MAJOCCHI: Very softly; she came to my bedside, looked and passed on.

ATTORNEY-GENERAL: How long did she remain in Bergami's room?

MAJOCCHI: About ten or fifteen minutes.

When the Attorney-General sat down, Brougham rose to cross examine.

BROUGHAM: Was it not a very severe accident Bergami met with?

MAJOCCHI: Yes.

BROUGHAM: He was much hurt?

MAJOCCHI: Yes, he could not ride.

BROUGHAM: Were you not taken into the service of the Princess to attend Bergami in his illness?

MAJOCCHI: Yes.

BROUGHAM: You have said he could not ride. Could he walk?

MAJOCCHI: I don't know.

BROUGHAM: Did he go out walking?

MAJOCCHI: I don't know whether he could walk.

BROUGHAM: Did you ever see him walking?

MAJOCCHI: I—I—don't remember. Non mi ricordo.

BROUGHAM: Was he attended by any medical man?

MAJOCCHI: Non mi ricordo.

BROUGHAM: Did you see Her Royal Highness go into the room of Hieronymus when *he* met with an accident?

MAJOCCHI: Non mi ricordo.

BROUGHAM: Have you not seen her go to Sir William Gell's room when he, too, was confined by illness?

MAJOCCHI: Non mi ricordo.

BROUGHAM: Was it not her constant practice to go into the apartment of any of her suite who happened to be ill to see after their health and their treatment?

MAJOCCHI: Non mi ricordo.

BROUGHAM: You were never ill yourself at Naples?

MAJOCCHI: Non mi ricordo.

BROUGHAM: Did the Princess make any difference between the highest and the lowest of her servants during any illness of any of them?

ATTORNEY-GENERAL: I object to this mode of pursuing the cross-examination. It is assuming that some of them were ill, of which there is no proof.

BROUGHAM: Then I will put the question another way, for I mean to assume nothing. Were all the servants in Her Majesty's suite always in perfect health, except Bergami during his illness from the kick of a horse?

MAJOCCHI: Non mi ricordo.

And so the farce continued, justifying completely Brougham's final and devastating comment: 'I have heard it asserted that the great prevailing feature of Majocchi's evidence, his lack of memory, signified but little because memories differ. They do. So does honesty. It will be my duty to point out parts of Majocchi's evidence in which I defy the wit of man to conceive any stronger or more palpable instances of false swearing than can be traced in the words "Non mi ricordo." I shall put it to Your Lordships that while Majocchi's testimony has abounded in guilty forgetfulness, no single example supporting the idea of an innocent forgetfulness has occurred.'

Another important witness was Louisa Demont, a one-time chamber-maid of Caroline's. 'She is the smartest dressed of *femmes de chambre*, but neither the youngest nor the prettiest,' an observer noted. 'In complexion she is a brunette; her cheeks sunk and shrivelled and her eye more remarkable for an expression of cunning than of intellect. She advanced to the bar with a degree of confidence which even the penetrating glance of Mr Brougham, who eyed her most perseveringly "from top to toe," did not at all affect.'

Brougham left the cross-examination to the junior counsel, John Williams, and a portion of it throws a light on the government methods. The Mr Powell referred to was a member of the Milan Commission.

WILLIAMS: You entered the service of the Princess in the year 1814?

DEMONT: Yes.

WILLIAMS: And remained in it until the year 1817?

DEMONT: Yes.

WILLIAMS: Did you quit the Princess's service of your own accord or were you discharged?

DEMONT: I was discharged.

WILLIAMS: Were you not discharged for saying something which you afterwards admitted to be false.

DEMONT: Yes.

WILLIAMS: You were applied to by some person or other soon after you were discharged from the Princess's service?

DEMONT: Yes, nearly one year after I had left her service.

WILLIAMS: To know what you had to say with respect to the Princess? Is that not so?

DEMONT: Yes.

WILLIAMS: Where were you examined?

DEMONT: At Milan.

WILLIAMS: How many examined you?

DEMONT: Four.

WILLIAMS: Was Mr Powell one?

DEMONT: Yes.

WILLIAMS: You have been thirteen months in England?

DEMONT: Yes.

WILLIAMS: Were you ever in England before?

DEMONT: No.

WILLIAMS: Have you finally agreed what you are to have for your evidence?

DEMONT: They have promised me nothing for my evidence.

WILLIAMS: No benefit or profit of any kind?

DEMONT: I expect no profit for coming here.

WILLIAMS: You do not believe, upon your oath, that you are to receive any money or benefit of any kind for coming to England?

DEMONT: I expect no advantage from coming here, only that they pay my expenses back to Switzerland.

WILLIAMS: Did Mr Powell examine you at any time in England?

DEMONT: No.

WILLIAMS: Has he not seen you frequently since your arrival in England?

DEMONT: He has not seen me often.

WILLIAMS: Has he seen you a dozen times since your arrival in England?

DEMONT: Yes, more.

WILLIAMS: Twenty, perhaps?

DEMONT: I do not know how often.

WILLIAMS: It was not upon the subject of this evidence you have given that he visited you?

DEMONT: No.

WILLIAMS: Did he never speak to you on the subject of this evidence?

DEMONT: No.

WILLIAMS: What? During those twenty visits, more or less, you had no talk whatever with him on the subject of your evidence?

DEMONT: I cannot say he said nothing about it, because I do not remember.

WILLIAMS: Have you ever said that the Princess was surrounded by spies in Italy?

DEMONT: I do not remember.

WILLIAMS: Or represented it in any manner?

DEMONT: I do not remember.

WILLIAMS: Will you swear you have not?

DEMONT: I will not swear, but I do not remember.

WILLIAMS (showing a letter to Demont casually and

then folding it so that only the signature is seen and holding it near her): Is that your writing?

DEMONT: It is not exactly like my writing.

WILLIAMS: Do you believe it to be your writing or not?

DEMONT: It is not exactly like my writing.

WILLIAMS: Do you believe it to be your writing—yes or no?

DEMONT: I do not think it is exactly my handwriting.

WILLIAMS: Do you believe it to be your handwriting— yes or no?

DEMONT: I cannot decide whether it is my handwriting. It is not quite like it.

WILLIAMS: Do you believe it—yes or no?

DEMONT: I cannot say yes or no, because it is not exactly like my handwriting.

WILLIAMS: Do you believe it to be your writing?

DEMONT: I cannot tell what to answer. I cannot answer to a thing of which I am not sure.

SOLICITOR-GENERAL: The paper is held so that she can only see part of the writing. The question can therefore only refer to the part which she sees.

WILLIAMS: I want her to prove or to disprove her handwriting, with respect to any given part of the paper. (He refolds the letter lengthwise.) You can now see the first half of every line clearly, can you not?

DEMONT: Yes.

WILLIAMS: Is that your handwriting?

DEMONT: I cannot tell exactly.

WILLIAMS: Was it not in the month of November, 1817, that you quitted the service of the Princess?

DEMONT: Yes.

WILLIAMS: Of course, at that time, you knew all the things about the Princess that you have been deposing these last two days before their Lordships?

DEMONT: Yes.

WILLIAMS: After you left her service but before you saw Mr Powell at Milan, did you never represent the character of the Princess to be of a very high description?

DEMONT: I do not remember.

WILLIAMS: Do you remember having said or written or represented that if the Princess could read your heart she would be convinced of the infinite respect, the unlimited attachment and the perfect affection you entertained for her august person?

DEMONT: I recollect I have written several times to my sister, but I do not remember the contents of my letters.

WILLIAMS: Will you swear that you did not write to your sister to that effect after you were discharged?

DEMONT: I have written to my sister.

WILLIAMS (reading): Have you not written to your sister: 'How often in a numerous circle have I with enthusiasm enumerated her rare talents, her mildness, her patience, her charity; in short all the perfections she possesses in so eminent a degree! How often have I seen my hearers affected and heard them exclaim that the world is unjust to cause so much unhappiness to one who deserves it so little?'

DEMONT: I do not remember whether I used those expressions.

WILLIAMS: But you admit to the sense?

DEMONT: Yes.

WILLIAMS: Do you not remember writing to this effect

or these words: 'You know that when the Princess is my subject I am not barren, for my journal is embellished with the effusion of my heart, my greatest desire having always been that the Princess should appear to be what she really is and that full justice should be rendered to her.' Do you remember having written to that effect?

DEMONT: I recollect that I wrote very often to my sister and spoke of Her Royal Highness.

WILLIAMS: And to this effect?

DEMONT: I do not remember.

WILLIAMS: Will you swear you did not?

DEMONT: No.

WILLIAMS (taking out another letter and pausing): Did you not write this to your sister? Listen carefully: 'I had almost forgotten to tell you a thing which will surprise you as much as it has done me. I was taking some refreshment at Aunt Clara's when I was informed that an unknown person wished to deliver me a letter and that he could trust it to no one else. I went downstairs and asked him to come up to my room. Imagine my astonishment when I broke the seal. A proposal was made to me to set off to London under the pretence of being a governess: I was promised high protection and a brilliant fortune in a short time. The letter was without signature; but to assure me of the truth of it, I was informed I might draw on a banker for as much money as I wished.'

SOLICITOR-GENERAL: I have not interposed when the counsel against the Bill asked about particular expressions used by the witness; but now that he is reading a letter, I feel it necessary to submit that the

74

regular course is for him to put it in the hand of the witness and to ask whether it is her handwriting or not.

WILLIAMS (giving the letter to Demont): Is that your handwriting?

DEMONT: Yes.

WILLIAMS: The whole of the letter to the end?

DEMONT: Yes.

WILLIAMS: You swear that?

DEMONT: Yes.

Mr Creevey, writing his daily account of the trial, noted: 'The *chienne* Demont turns out everything one could wish on her cross-examination. A most infernally damaging day for the prosecution.' There were to be three more such days before, on September 4, Guiseppe Rastelli appeared at the bar of the House to give the evidence which was to be the *coup de grâce*.

Rastelli was obviously nervous. He gave his evidence in so low a voice that Thomas Denman, Caroline's Solicitor-General, intervened: 'Speak louder, sir: we must hear your voice as well as the interpreter's!'

After establishing Rastelli's identity, the King's Solicitor-General asked: 'Did you ever see Bergami ride out in any carriage with the Princess?'

'Several times.'

'Describe how they were seated.'

'She was seated on Bergami's knees.'

'Do you remember Bergami's sometimes wearing a cloak?'

'Yes, a cloak that was a present.'

'How have you seen it placed?'

'I have seen the Princess extend it over herself and Bergami also, so as to cover Bergami with it.'

'Was it your duty to accompany the carriage on horseback?'

'It was my duty to ride in front and to come near the carriage when I was called to or sent for.'

'Do you recollect any particular occasion when you went near the carriage?'

'I once went near the carriage to enquire what road I should take.'

'Was the carriage open?'

'It was.'

'When you came near the carriage, what did you observe?'

Rastelli described what he observed and added that he was so ashamed that he turned away.

There was a sensation in the House at this first-hand account which could leave no shadow of doubt that Caroline and Bergami were on intimate terms. One of the Peers, thinking that he had misheard, asked that the questions and answers should be read over by the shorthand-writer.

Denman immediately rose to cross-examine. He suggested that Rastelli had been dismissed from Caroline's service for theft and, when the witness denied it, persisted: 'You never said to anybody that you had been dismissed on the charge of stealing corn?'

'I have not,' said Rastelli, 'because I never told a lie.'

Denman turned on the interpreter: 'Does he mean to say he never told a lie or that he never told a lie without being well paid for it?'

There were cries of 'Order! Order!' and the King's Solicitor-General appealed to the Lord Chancellor against the question. But, considering the state of indignation in the House, the Lord Chancellor over-ruled the objection.

'Do you understand English?' Denman asked Rastelli.

'Not at all.'

Then, suddenly, Denman snapped unexpectedly: 'How long have you been in England?'

'Since the day before yesterday.'

A hush fell on the House as Denman proceeded to underline the oddity of the sudden visit by establishing that for the last two years Rastelli had been a most active agent of the Milan Commission, gathering the 'Green Bag' evidence and posting over Europe with it.

'When you left Milan, did you bring your father with you and your wife and your children?'

'I did not.'

'What are you to have for coming?'

'They have promised me nothing.'

'What do you expect to have?'

'Nothing. They have promised me nothing. I have nothing to expect.'

'You mean that you expect nothing?'

'Yes.'

Denman then returned to the episode in the carriage. 'You came back for orders, did you?' he asked.

'I did.'

'When you had not received your orders on setting out, you were in the habit of coming back to the carriage in order to receive them?'

'Not always. They had given me their orders before we set out and on this occasion they thought they would be sufficient.'

'Did they call you to the carriage?'

'No. They did not hear me. I went of my own accord.'

'To whom did you first tell this story?'

'I never told it before except to the Commission.'

'How long was that after you saw it?'

'About eleven months or a year afterwards perhaps.'

'Just tell us in what month it was.'

'I don't know precisely.'

Brougham's comment on this when later he opened the defence was pertinent enough: 'When Rastelli swore to scenes too disgusting to be detailed, he had never opened his mouth on the subject. His lips had been hermetically sealed until he was called on by the Commission at Milan. Through ten long months that witness was silent. Is it credible he could have been so reserved if he had anything to tell? Is there one, even among your Lordships, whose lips are schooled to enact the courtier even when no court is present, who would not have repeated it to someone or other? Yet this low person never mentioned a syllable to any living person? But I shall not admit that he concealed these extraordinary things for days, weeks or even hours. I believe he concealed it from the time of his hearing that others had been liberally paid for slanders and resolved to imitate their example.' For the defence did not know, any more than the people knew, the real circumstances of Rastelli's entering Caroline's service. But the people, at least, estimated his evidence at its true worth.

Two days after Rastelli's evidence, Creevey could write: 'This bill will never pass. My belief is that it will be abandoned on the adjournment. The entire middle order of people are against it and are daily becoming more critical of the King and the Lords for carrying on this prosecution.' He was wrong about the abandonment, but on the day before the adjournment, he had to report: 'The Queen went down the river yesterday. I saw her pass the House of Commons on the deck of her state barge. . . . Erskine, who was afterwards at Blackfriars Bridge, said he was sure there were 200,000 people collected to see her. . . . There was not a single vessel in the river that did not hoist their colours and man their yards for her, and it is with the greatest difficulty that the watermen on the Thames are kept from destroying the hulk which lies off the House of Commons to protect the witnesses.'

The defence opened on October 3. 'You can form no conception of the rage of the Lords at Brougham fixing this time,' Creevey wrote. 'It interferes with everything —pheasant shooting, Newmarket, etc., etc. . . . He has performed miracles and the reasons he has just been giving me for fixing the time he has done show his understanding (if one doubted it) to be of the very first order.' Handicapped, as he was, by his ignorance of the real circumstances of the Government intrigues, Henry Brougham had indeed made an almost miraculous attack and in the days that followed his opening of the defence, this forty-two-year-old Edinburgh lawyer, son of a Scottish manse, who from the depths of his soul hated and despised the accusers of the Queen he had served for eleven years, kept his ear very close to the ground. And on Friday, October 13, he was able to bring the prosecution crashing to ruin.

In a deceptively quiet and courteous voice, he asked the King's Attorney-General: 'I wish to know of my learned friend whether we can have access to Rastelli. Is he here? Is he in this country?'

The King's Attorney-General stretched across the

79

Bar and answered Brougham in a very low voice that no one could hear.

The Lord Chancellor gave the Crown counsel time to think by leaving the House for a few moments.

On his return, Brougham, in a voice which echoed round the Chamber, said: 'My Lords, I wish Rastelli to be called.'

'If my learned friend wishes to call Rastelli,' said the King's Attorney-General, 'he can certainly call him.'

'I wish to know,' roared Brougham, 'if Rastelli is in the country and, if in the country, where he is?'

The House was tense. The Lord Chancellor could delay no longer. 'Mr Attorney,' he said, 'is Rastelli here?'

The King's Attorney-General realized that Brougham had outmanœuvred him. The answer could no longer be evaded. 'No,' he said, 'he has been sent to Milan.'

'Then,' said Brougham, his long arms waving in their characteristic angular fashion, 'I wish to know whether I am obliged to go on with this Bill?'

The King's Attorney-General stumbled through explanations . . . Rastelli had been sent to Milan with dispatches . . . there was no idea that he would be wanted again as he had already been cross-examined . . . he had gone to assure the relatives of the witnesses that those witnesses were indeed safe and sound from the indignation of the London mobs . . .

Brougham refused to argue. 'If witnesses are allowed to leave the country during the proceedings,' he said, 'there is an end to the security which Your Lordships think you possess that no perjury shall be permitted with impunity at your Bar. I ask again, am I obliged in these circumstances to go on with the case?'

Lord Holland sprang to his feet and moved that counsel withdrew from the House. When they had done so, he addressed his fellow Peers: 'I rise to state on behalf of Your Lordships and the cause of justice that the fact that has just come out is absolutely monstrous.'

He was interrupted by a cry of approval which even the cold language of the official report describes in parenthesis: 'Loud cries of "Hear! Hear!" from both sides of the House re-echoed for many moments.'

'Gracious God,' Holland continued when the noise died away, 'can Your Lordships suppose that after such a proceeding as this we are safe from the suspicion that must be cast upon us?' (Loud cheers.) 'Here is Rastelli, who stated one of the most disgusting things heard in a court of justice—a man on whom suspicion now rests that he has been engaged in suborning witnesses for the prosecution, not merely escaping, but being sent away by the Government. If Your Lordships submit to being dragged through the mire in this matter, you will taint this branch of the legislature. Considering these circumstances as forming a *prima facie* case of the existence of a conspiracy to pervert justice, Your Lordships will do well to get rid of the disgust and fatigue of this infamous proceeding.'

The Lords insisted on themselves examining the Government agent who had engineered Rastelli's return, but when Lord Holland asked him to produce a letter concerning it, he refused, saying that he did not consider himself at liberty to produce it, 'being as I am, a man confidentially employed.'

This gave Brougham his second great opportunity. He could now carry the war into the enemy's country.

81

'With the permission of Your Lordships I wish to ask the witness who is his employer in this case?'

It was a master-stroke. At last he had forced into the open, as nearly as he dared within the Constitution, what indeed everyone knew but none could say—that the proceedings were nothing but George's personal vendetta against Caroline. Feverishly the Government Peers tried to rule his question out of order, but he persisted and began the speech which, of all speeches George, who was becoming increasingly touchy on the subject of his obesity and his curious shape, never forgot or forgave.

'My Lords,' said Brougham, 'I consider it essential that this question should be put. This is the first witness who can give us the important information which I now seek. To whom are we opposed? When we are acquainted with the unknown, the interesting unknown, we may trace its actions and its conduct and bring from its own mouth—if it have a mouth—who and what he is. I know nothing of this shapeless being, if shape it can be called.'

His hands outlined the shape, but even the dullest of their Lordships, noticing the suppressed laughter of those who had seen the point, had begun to realize who the 'shape' was.

'I know nothing about this retiring phantom, this uncertain shape,' Brougham continued,

' "If shape it might be called that shape had none
Distinguishable in finger, joint or limb"

And such, Your Lordships will admit, "that shadow seemed for each seemed either" and

"what seemed his head
The likeness of a kingly crown had on."

82

Yet under this shape, this "airy nothing" I am to face the adverse party. I am to be met at every turn in the proceedings by not being able to put a single question to this visionary personage. I am to pursue this shape——'

But, of course, it could not be allowed. The Lord Chancellor called the gale of guffaws to order and told Mr Brougham he could not continue his quest.

Nevertheless, the case was won. Though the trial dragged on for three more weeks, the conclusion was foregone. The Bill indeed passed its Third Reading, but only by a majority of nine and those nine were the Archbishop of Canterbury and eight obliging Bishops. The Government abandoned the Bill.

As this was announced by the Prime Minister, Lord Liverpool, in the House, a supporter of the Queen met her 'coming out alone from her waiting-room, preceded by an usher. She had a dazed look, more tragical than consternation. The usher pushed open the folding doors of the great staircase and she began to descend. She was all shuddering and she took hold of the banister, pausing for a moment. That sudden clutch with which she caught the railing was as if her hand had been a skinless heart.'

Outside, when the news was known, there was at first 'a kind of stupor.' Then, according to one who was there, 'everyone instantly between Charing Cross and Whitehall, turned and came rushing down, filling Old and New Palace Yards, as if a deluge were unsluiced. The generous exultation of the people was beyond all description.'

On that fantastic evening London went mad and Caroline was cheered and toasted as no hero had ever been. But her great moment was in the little retiring-room at the House, where she had spent so much time during the trial quietly playing backgammon in preference to hearing herself slandered.

Here she thanked Brougham and Denman and signed a document they had brought her. After she had written 'Caroline,' she returned the pen to Brougham. Then, suddenly, she asked for it again and added in a firm hand 'Regina' to her signature, saying as she did so: 'Caroline Regina, in spite of them all.'

But George said that he would rather die or lose his crown than submit to any compromise of any sort with her and swore that she should never be crowned.

In due course she was officially notified that 'His Majesty having determined that the Queen shall form no part of the ceremonial of his coronation, it is there-fore the Royal pleasure that the Queen shall not attend the said ceremony.' In the circumstances, it became a necessary point of honour for her to be in Westminster Abbey on Coronation Day, July 19, 1821. And now not only the country but the Government were divided. Until five in the evening of July 18, the Government had not decided whether to obey the King or to resign.

The two people who had no doubts about what to do were George and Caroline. George spent the previous night barricaded in the Speaker's House in Old Palace Yard, a stone's throw from the Abbey; Caroline, hoping to take everyone by surprise, arrived at the Abbey at 5.30 in the morning.

But she found all entrances closed against her. One door was banged in her face. The crowds, which had been dense since midnight, watched the scene and even the occupants of the expensive seats 'applauded her loudly in most places.' Some one pointed out an opening to the platform by which she could gain the covered way leading to Poets' Corner.

At this last door, Lord Hood, who was in attendance on her, demanded admission. The door-keepers requested to see her ticket.

'I present to you your Queen,' said Lord Hood. 'Surely it is not necessary for her to have a ticket.'

'My orders are specific and I feel bound to obey them,' replied the door-keeper.

Caroline laughed and Lord Hood drew from his pocket a Peer's ticket for one person.

'This,' said the door-keeper, 'will let one person pass and no more.'

Lord Hood passed the ticket to the Queen, but she refused to go in without her attendants, since no provision had been made for accommodating her. She would go only as Queen and without a ticket.

'You refuse the Queen admission,' said Lord Hood.

'We only act in conformity with our orders,' answered the unhappy door-keeper.

So Caroline returned to her carriage and drove back to South Audley Street, accompanied by a tremendous concourse of people who broke the windows of all the houses on the route which had 'G.R.' or other decorations in them and, on passing Carlton House, were thunderous with groans and hisses.

Her attendants urged Caroline to rest after the strain and her equerry was able to record during the morning: 'Her Majesty is gone to bed while the better and stronger half is in the act of getting crowned.'

Caroline, however, had no intention of repining. A few nights later Denman found her with a large party, dancing and laughing even though 'her spirits were frightfully overstrained.'

At Drury Lane the following week Kean's performance of *Othello* was turned into a demonstration in her favour. Every passage that could be construed as an allusion to her case was received with plaudits and when Emilia made her outburst about the 'odious, damned lie,' a voice from the audience cried out: 'O what Iagos have beset the Queen' and was received with applause from every part of the theatre.

Caroline decided herself to see Kean's *Richard III* on Monday, July 30 and though, during the performance, she felt unwell she stayed till the end. On Tuesday a doctor diagnosed internal inflammation.

A week later she was dead.

One circumstance of her quick illness, from which she predicted she would not recover, was memorable. When Denman suggested sending a messenger to Italy to seal up her papers lest they fell into her enemies' hands, she said: 'What if they do? They can find nothing, because there is nothing and never has been to impeach my character.'

Caroline's funeral provided a last occasion for a triumphant demonstration in her favour. Authority decided that the cortege to Harwich (for she was to be buried in her native Brunswick) must on no account be allowed to pass through the City of London. She had died at her residence, Brandenburgh House, in Hammersmith and it had been ordered that at Kensington the procession should turn off the main road, through Church Street, to Bayswater Road and then north up Edgware Road. Londoners decided otherwise.

An enormous barricade of overturned waggons and other impediments blocked the entrance to Church Street and the procession was halted while messengers were sent to the Prime Minister for instructions. A troop of Life Guards was sent, with orders to divert the procession through the Park and gain Edgware Road by way of what is now Marble Arch. But the populace closed the Park gates and clung to them so that, without a massacre, they could not be opened. For a second time the authorities had to give in and for the third time the crowd forestalled them and threw up another barrier at the bottom of Park Lane.

This time the procession was made to turn back and the Hyde Park Gate opened, so that the cortege could pass but the people were excluded. The crowd thereupon made for Cumberland Gate (Marble Arch), tore down the railings and used them for weapons, and attacked the soldiers with brickbats and stones. The troops opened fire, killing two and wounding several more and, for the moment, the planned route up Edgware Road, along the New Road (Marylebone Road and Euston Road) was followed. But at Tottenham Court Road there was another impassable barricade and once more the people had their way, driving the procession down Drury Lane and so into the City by Temple Bar. The people having thus gained the victory, the body was taken triumphantly through the City. The Lord Mayor was forced to leave a meeting and come rapidly to Temple Bar to receive the cortege, which, with him now at its head, passed through streets where all the shops were closed, the windows crowded with citizens for the most part dressed in deep mourning and the streets full of orderly crowds which 'exceeded all calculation.'

So, in triumph, the 'Injured Queen of England'—the words were inscribed on the coffin—left the capital for the last time.

The story of Caroline remains mysterious. The old question: Was she innocent or guilty? is, indeed, no longer to be asked. There can be no serious doubt of her innocence of the charges brought against her at her trial. But her sudden, unexpected and most convenient death provokes inevitable speculation, especially when considered in the context of the political ferment of the time and the undisguised relief with which George regarded it.

But, above all, there is the mystery of George's conduct. The depths to which he stooped in his efforts to get rid of Caroline and to humiliate her are altogether disproportionate to the apparent causes and inappropriate to his basic character. And the solution, I suggest, is to be found in the persons of William Austin and Maria Fitzherbert. Because of the menace of the first, George was forced in 1806 to find Caroline 'innocent' when she was 'guilty' and in 1820 to try to prove her guilty when she was innocent. Because of the status of the second, who was his true and only wife, he could not, without violating the ultimate decencies, allow his State-wife, (who was no wife even though she might claim to be the mother of a legal 'Prince of Wales') to be crowned.

It is probable that the now-inaccessible papers removed to Windsor in 1935 contain much enlightenment on both these points. Even without them, we know so much more than the crowds of 1820 knew that it is impossible to withhold admiration that, despite their almost total ignorance, their instincts were so sound.

The circumstances may at least provoke the reader, even though he cannot answer these questions, to ask a larger and more important question: 'What is "History"?'

2

THE PARENTAGE OF
QUEEN ELIZABETH I

JANE DORMER, friend, companion and lady-in-waiting
of Queen Mary Tudor, left it on record that Mary
would never call Elizabeth sister 'nor be persuaded she
was her father's daughter. She would say she had the
face and countenance of Mark Smeaton.'

As no portrait exists of Mark Smeaton, who was tried
and executed for adultery with Elizabeth's mother,
Anne Boleyn, we have no means of forming our own
judgment on the likeness; but at least we can see that
there is little resemblance between Elizabeth and her
presumed father, Henry VIII. Elizabeth seems to have
been, in appearance, very much her mother's daughter.
She had Anne's nose with startling exactitude, Anne's
mouth and forehead, Anne's high cheek-bones and
pointed chin. As Anne's eyes were said by observers to
be 'black and beautiful,' so were Elizabeth's. But
Elizabeth's exquisite hands, of which she was very
proud and which all who saw her mentioned as of out-
standing beauty, were not her mother's nor had they
anything in common with the pudgy coarseness of
Henry VIII's. Her hair is supposed to have been like
the King's—reddish, as Mary's was—but it must be
remembered that Elizabeth was totally bald before she
was thirty and that the reddish wigs that she wore for

forty-two of her forty-five years as Queen were intended to create precisely that impression.

As in appearance, so in character. Elizabeth's could hardly be better described than in that passage in which Paul Friedman, in his standard biography of Anne Boleyn, sums up her mother: 'She was incredibly vain, ambitious, unscrupulous, coarse, fierce and relentless. . . . Her virtues, such as they were, were her own. So we may pass no harsher judgment on her than was passed by Cromwell when, speaking confidentially to Chapuis of the woman whose destruction he had wrought, he could not refrain from extolling her courage and intelligence. Among her good qualities he might also have included her warm and constant attachment to her friends.'

Elizabeth's chief accomplishments were music and dancing. Even when she was fifty-six, six or seven galliards a morning, besides music and singing, were her custom. And in earlier days—she was thirty-one—one of her questions to Melville, Mary Queen of Scots' envoy, was whether Mary played well on the lute and virginals. When Melville answered: 'Reasonably for a Queen,' he was allowed to hear her playing 'exceedingly well' on the virginals and was detained an extra day to watch her dance, at which he was bound to admit that the Queen of Scots 'danced not so high and disposedly as she did.'

Mark Smeaton was a dancer and Court musician.

It seems, therefore, not altogether pointless to consider the implications of Dr Ortiz's information to the Emperor on May 23, 1536 about what he had heard in Rome—that 'in order to have a son who might be attributed to the King, she [Anne] committed adultery with a singer who taught her to play on instruments.'

As Smeaton's unwavering admission of guilt before, during and after his trial is of little evidential value because he was tortured, it is best to start the enquiry by examining the strength of Mary Tudor's belief that Elizabeth was not her sister. How tenaciously did she hold it?

[i] Mary and Elizabeth

The dominating factor of European politics during the reign of Mary Tudor was the rivalry between France and Spain. Compared with these two powers, England and Scotland were little more than pawns which must be preserved from falling into the rival's hands, or moved so as not to obstruct the greater pieces' advance. And as Scotland 'belonged' (in this sense) to France, so England 'belonged' to Spain. Mary Stuart, Queen, from her infancy, of Scotland, had been sent to France when she was six to be brought up at the French court until the time came when, at sixteen, she was to marry the Dauphin. She was twelve when Philip of Spain married Mary Tudor, Queen of England, and so brought England into the rival orbit.

But Mary Queen of Scots was also Mary Tudor's heir, since Elizabeth, born while Henry VIII's true wife, Catherine of Aragon, was still alive had been declared illegitimate both by the Pope and (temporarily) by Henry VIII and the obedient English Parliament.

Thus the one object of Philip of Spain, while he was King-Consort of England (from 1554 to 1558) was to prevent at all costs the succession of Mary Queen of Scots to the English throne, should he and Mary Tudor have no issue. He wished to ensure this by marrying Elizabeth to his first cousin, Emmanuel of Savoy, while at the same time persuading Mary to recognize her as her heir.

This, in the circumstances, should have been the easiest of things to accomplish. Mary was an infatuated wife who would do anything, it seemed, that he asked. For Philip's sake, she brought England into war on the Spanish side, which lost Calais, the last English possession in France. She gave him freely of her money. She endured his interminable-seeming absences. But this one thing she would not do. She would neither allow Elizabeth's marriage nor proclaim her her heir, because these actions violated her conscience. Believing her not to be her sister, she would do nothing which could imply that she was.

In doing this she was acting against her own interest, for as long as Elizabeth remained in England and unmarried, she was the centre of all pro-French intrigue, and a perpetual danger to the Queen. As the Spanish Ambassador noted in the last year of the reign: 'Elizabeth was brought up in the doctrines of the new religion, she was formerly of the French faction, she hates the Queen. . . . All the plots and disorders that have troubled England during the last four years have been aimed at placing its government in Elizabeth's hands sooner than the course of nature would permit, as witness the actions of Peter Carew, the Duke of Suffolk, Courtenay, Dudley, the Frenchman Berthe-ville, Stafford and others, in which affairs the French and Elizabeth were involved.'

94

Thus it would have been to Mary's own advantage and safety to have arranged Elizabeth's marriage, quite apart from the consideration of pleasing Philip. But she could not do it. Her simplicity and honesty—even Pollard admits that 'she was the most honest of the Tudors'—and the deep religious faith which made her, if anything, over-scrupulous in matters of conscience forbade that concession.

The Duke of Savoy first visited England in the December of the year in which Philip and Mary were married, 1554. Mary received him with every courtesy, gave him the Garter, put Somerset House at his disposal—but refused to let him see Elizabeth. Events on the Continent recalled him after a very short stay so that it was not until 1556 that the matter of the marriage became practical politics.

At the beginning of 1557, rumours were abroad that Mary had given her consent and that the marriage had been arranged. 'The King of France has heard with great regret that negotiations are going on for a match between the Duke of Savoy and the Lady Elizabeth,' wrote Simon Renard to Philip. 'They say that the Queen has given her consent. . . . They intend to move to declare that the Lady Elizabeth is a bastard, hoping thus to upset Your Majesty's plans.' But the news of Mary's consent was false and it was she who was considering having Elizabeth declared a bastard by Act of Parliament and debarred from the succession.

Philip, from Brussels, wrote an angry letter to his wife charging her, on her conscience, to consent to the marriage which would be for the good of the Catholic cause in Europe. She had already been taken to task by one of his religious advisers who, Mary said, 'propounded questions so obscure that, to my simple understanding, there was no comprehending them: as for instance: "Who was King in Adam's days?" and said, withal, "that I was bound to conclude this marriage by an article in my creed." ' 'I beg in all humility,' she wrote, 'that Your Highness will defer this matter till your return and then it will be manifest whether I am culpable or not. Otherwise I shall live in apprehension of Your Highness's displeasure, which would be worse to me than death; for I have already begun to taste it too much to my regret.'

The crucial passage in this long letter runs: 'I will say nothing now except, seeing you hold that I should examine my conscience to know if it is in conformity with the truth or no, to supplicate Your Highness most humbly to name and appoint what persons you judge fit to speak with me about this affair, *for that which my conscience holds, it has held these four and twenty years.*' It was twenty-four years since Elizabeth's birth. The passage in italics is omitted in the Protestant historian, John Strype's *Ecclesiastical Memorials* and subsequent historians who have copied him.

Philip sent his confessor, de Fresneda, to persuade Mary 'for the safety and quiet of the Kingdom and religion, lest Elizabeth, feeling herself spurned should ... take an anti-Spanish husband, to give her the hope of the succession.' But Mary remained adamant and, according to the Venetian Ambassador—whose secret service was excellent—she obstinately maintained that Elizabeth was neither her sister nor the daughter of King Henry, nor would she hear of favouring her.'

Philip himself came to England in March and was

followed shortly by the Duchess of Lorraine who was to take Elizabeth back with her for the marriage. But, despite everything, Mary would not give way and at the beginning of May the Duchess returned to the Continent without Elizabeth.

During this last visit of Philip to his wife, from March till July, 1557, the matter must have been settled privately between them, for thereafter the project was quietly dropped. But in the spring of the following year, another suitor appeared. Philip's special envoy to Mary, Count Feria, reported it. 'An ambassador of the King of Sweden came here recently. Several days passed without his having audience of the Queen or even demanding it. His mission appears to consist of two parts: one about commercial affairs between England and Sweden and the other to negotiate a match between the Lady Elizabeth and the King of Sweden's son, for which purpose he brought a letter from the young man accrediting him to the Lady. Before he had been received by the Queen, he went to present his letter to the Lady Elizabeth. . . . When this ambassador first arrived, the Queen was greatly distressed, thinking that Your Majesty would blame her because the proposed match a year ago [with Savoy] had not come off. Now that the Lady Elizabeth has answered that she does not wish to marry, the Queen has calmed down; but she takes a most passionate interest in the affair. She now realizes that her pregnancy has come to nothing and seems afraid Your Majesty will urge her to take a decision [about marrying off Elizabeth]. Figueroa and I think Your Majesty ought to do this, grasping the occasion supplied by this ambassador and the pregnancy matter. . . . I do not think the Queen will wish to prevent

Elizabeth from succeeding, in case God grants no issue to Your Majesties.'

Mary dealt with the matter in her own way. She summoned the Swedish ambassador, told him that, after having committed such a breach of etiquette as to deliver a letter to her sister before presenting his credentials, he had better go home and never return with such a message, and curtly dismissed him. Yet, in spite of her realization that, if Elizabeth had to marry, Savoy would have been the match dictated by interests of religion, as Philip had insisted, Mary still would not recognize Elizabeth as her sister. She knew now that all hope of her own child-bearing was gone; she was desperately sick (she had in fact only five more months to live); yet, not until nine days before her death, when eaten with cancer and exhausted with a fever, she was unable even to read a letter, did she yield to the importunities of her Councillors, badgering her round her bed, and name Elizabeth her successor.

She had kept her conscience in the matter, against all odds, clear to the end.

In face of these facts, it seems to me impossible to deny that, whoever Elizabeth's father may have been, Mary believed that he was Mark Smeaton, as she told Jane Dormer; and for this belief she had reasons which, in her own mind, could not be shaken. Against her inclination, against her self-interest, against her love for her husband and against the cause of the religion that was so dear to her, she took the only course she considered compatible with 'that which held her conscience for four and twenty years.' What proof she had, we cannot know; but, judging by events, it seems to have convinced Philip when at last she told him of it.

According to Girolamo Pollini, whose *L'Historia Ecclesiastica della Rivoluzion d'Inghilterra* was published in 1594, Mary 'was present assisting with the relatives and friends of Anne Boleyn in the lying-in chamber when Elizabeth was born; and there she heard, among the ladies and persons of court, such scandals relative to the conduct of the mother as made her declare that "she was sure the infant was not her sister." ' This would provide some basis for her belief, but it is unlikely in view of her later conduct that she had no surer grounds than what one historian has characterized as the 'evil reports' of 'malignant busybodies.' Mary at the time of Elizabeth's birth was seventeen and must have known Smeaton, who had been at Court as a favourite dancer and musician for some years.

[ii] St Thomas More

That Mary believed Elizabeth to be Smeaton's child is, obviously, taken by itself, no proof that she was so in fact; and the next evidence worth examining is a curious remark made by St Thomas More.

St Thomas More died a martyr for the Catholic faith on July 6, 1535, because he refused to acknowledge Henry VIII 'the supreme head on earth of the Church of England.' There was no doubt or equivocation about this on anyone's part and More himself put it beyond a peradventure when he described the Act of Supremacy which gave Henry and his successors this status, as 'an Act of Parliament directly repugnant to the laws of God and His Holy Church, the supreme government of which, or of any part thereof, may no temporal Prince presume by any law to take upon him, as rightfully belonging to the See of Rome, a spiritual pre-eminence by the mouth of our Saviour Himself, personally present upon earth, only to St Peter and his successors, bishops of the same See, by special prerogative granted.' He pointed out that 'this realm, being but one member and small part of the Church might not make a particular law disagreeable with the general law of Christ's universal Catholic Church, no more than the City of London, being but one poor member in respect of the whole realm, might make a law against an Act of Parliament to bind the whole realm' and that 'no more might this realm of England refuse obedience to the See of Rome than might the child refuse obedience to his own natural father.'

And on the scaffold he called the crowd 'to bear witness with him that he should now there suffer death in and for the faith of the Holy Catholic Church.'

Originally, in 1531, the King's claim to the Supremacy had been couched in the terms . . . 'of the Church and Clergy of England, whose especial Protector, single and supreme Lord and, as far as the law of Christ allows, even Supreme Head, we acknowledge His Majesty to be.' The saving clause 'as far as the law of Christ allows' meant that the oath could be taken by anyone without a violation of conscience. But in the November of 1534, after More had been in prison for six months, it was tightened and 'as far as the law of Christ allows' was omitted. Thus More was not arrested specifically on the grounds for which he was, in the end, martyred and canonized.

What led to More's imprisonment was his refusal to take the Oath of Succession, which he was asked to swear in the April of 1534—that is to say, seven months after Elizabeth's birth. A Succession Act was a constitutional innovation. This was the first ever passed to regulate the succession to the throne of England and it insisted among other things, that Henry's lawful heirs were his issue by Anne Boleyn. Protestant no less than Catholic writers have assumed that More's refusal to take the oath was based on the obvious ground that this would be to declare invalid Henry's marriage to Catherine of Aragon which the Pope had declared valid and thus to become implicated in the whole question of Papal jurisdiction. When Cranmer and Cromwell asked that More might be allowed to take the oath in a modified form, Henry, influenced by Anne Boleyn's 'importunate clamour,' refused on the ground that 'it might be taken not only as a confirmation of the Bishop of Rome's authority, but also as a reprobation of the King's second marriage.' Thus Henry, as well as later commentators, assumed that the implied theological issue could have constituted More's reason and that he resisted the oath (the penalty for which was imprisonment, not death) on the same—or at least similar—grounds of Faith, for which he ultimately and unequivocally died.

But did he?

It seems to me that not sufficient attention has been paid to a passage in a letter he wrote while in prison to Dr Nicholas Wilson who was also in prison for refusing the oath and, unsettled in mind, was asking More's advice. In the course of his answer, More wrote: 'As touching the oath, the causes for which I refused it, no man wotteth what they be, for they be secret in mine own conscience; some other, peradventure, than those that other men would ween and such as I never disclosed to any man yet, nor never intend to do while I live.'

This description hardly fits any of the reasons adduced which were precisely what 'other men would ween,' since the validity of Henry's first marriage and the relevance of the Papal condemnation were obstacles apparent to everyone. Nor can More's 'such as I never disclosed to any man yet nor never intend to do while I live' by any stretch of language or imagination be applied to the Royal Supremacy, which had already been a matter of three years' public argument and which, as we have seen, still contained, at that point, a 'conscience clause.'

More, as a statesman, a friend of King Henry's and Wolsey's successor as Lord Chancellor, was prepared to bow to authority as far as it was in conscience possible. Lord Acton, indeed, has blamed him for the lengths to which he carried his submission. He was even prepared to accept the Act of Succession as being within the competence of Parliament, provided he was not asked at the same time to recognize the Boleyn marriage. In the question of the divorce of Catherine, he had so scrupulously refused to 'meddle' that he asked one of Catherine's partisans not to call on him and told him that any letters he might receive he would feel bound in honour to show to the King. Yet against Anne Boleyn, he was immovable.

Months before there was any question of an Oath of Succession, he made a gesture which can only be construed as reflecting on her personally. Although he was a former Lord Chancellor and still a member of the Council, and as such, had a strictly official position, he refused to attend Anne's Coronation, when requested to do so by the Bishops of Durham, Bath and Winchester.

The motive which may have determined this refusal is thus defined by his latest biographer: 'The coronation was a religious act. . . . After the anointing Mass was said and the new Queen "kneeled before the altar where she received of the Archbishop the Holy Sacrament." This was something more than an act of state; it was the sanctification of a union made in defiance of the Pope who had not yet pronounced his decision on the validity of the marriage between Henry and Catherine. It may have been some such view of the matter that kept Thomas More away from the coronation.'*

It may indeed have been so, but such a theory seems to me reading history backwards by using knowledge of what More eventually died for and applying it to an earlier and different situation. Also it credits More, the lay statesman, accommodating to the utmost and anxious to obey the King, his benefactor and friend, with an outlook more in keeping with that of a bishop such as St John Fisher. Had the Pope already pronounced on the invalidity of the marriage of Henry and Anne Boleyn—which in fact he did not until five weeks after Anne's Coronation—the situation would have been radically different. As it was, it would surely have been more in keeping with all that we know of More for him to conform where nonconformity was not yet demanded and when he could plead, without stretching his conscience, the excuse of official duty.

His refusal seems to me to have been what Anne

* E. E. Reynolds: *Saint Thomas More*, p. 279.

considered it at the time—an action which reflected on her personally. And it would be explicable if More's secret 'such as I never disclosed unto any man yet nor never intend to do while I live' was that the child she was within three months of bearing was not Henry's. It would also have been consonant with his refusal ten months later to take the oath to Henry acknowledging the Royal succession was first to the sons of Anne 'and for fault of such sons of your body begotten . . . to the eldest issue female, which is the Lady Elizabeth.'

In any case, it is not too much to claim that More, by his own testimony, knew a secret which must never be spoken and which, in some way, concerned Elizabeth I's mother.

[iii] Anne Boleyn and Mark Smeaton

Anne Boleyn was tried, found guilty and executed in the May of 1536 on the charge 'that the Lady Anne Queen of England having been the wife of the king for the space of three years or more . . . did falsely and traitorously procure . . . divers of the king's daily and familiar servants to become her adulterers and con- cubines.'

Three of the men tried and executed as her lovers were Henry Noreys,* Gentleman of the King's

* There was a general rumour that Noreys was Elizabeth's father. Elizabeth when she was Queen showed excessive favour to Noreys's son; but it seems more likely that the implication of Noreys and Bryerton, as leading members of the Boleyn faction, was as much political as personal; and that Elizabeth's later close friendship with the younger Noreys was not because he was her brother, but because his father had been so chivalrous a champion of her mother.

Bedchamber, Keeper of his Privy Purse and one of his favourites; Sir Francis Weston, the son of the under-treasurer of the exchequer, who from being a royal page had risen to the rank of Gentleman of the Privy Chamber, had married a rich heiress and, at the coronation of Anne, had been created a Knight of the Bath; and William Bryerton, nephew of Sir William Bryerton (one of Henry's ablest captains) who, like Weston, had risen from page to Gentleman of the Privy Chamber.

All pleaded not guilty and there is every possibility that they were telling the truth. The jury had been carefully chosen, and, as Wolsey had once remarked: 'If the Crown were prosecutor and asserted it, juries would be found to bring in a verdict that Abel was the murderer of Cain.'

An attempt was made to save Sir Francis Weston, whose rich and powerful family had occasionally opposed the Boleyns; but this, even with the support of the French ambassador, was unsuccessful. Henry's minister, Thomas Cromwell, to keep in the good graces of the King (who was already courting Jane Seymour) had at all costs to get rid of Anne, and he had no intention of leaving a 'Boleyn faction' to trouble him after her execution.

That Anne was a loose woman and that she had had several lovers, is denied by no one; but that the actual charges against Noreys, Bryerton and Weston, as framed in the indictment, are true seems improbable. To quote Friedmann, 'even if it be admitted that Anne was one of the most depraved women of an extremely base court, it is most unlikely that she behaved in the manner described in the indictments.'

Even more unlikely—indeed the charge may be dismissed as preposterous—is the accusation of incest with her brother, George Viscount Rochford. The only evidence brought forward is that she was occasionally alone with him! In his case, the reason for his death is comprehensible enough. He was sufficiently intelligent and self-assertive to be a natural leader—was, in fact, already 'in opposition' to Cromwell and would never have rested till he had avenged his sister's death. He was also fatally indiscreet and had announced both that Henry was impotent and that Elizabeth was not the King's child.

At his trial, Rochford defended himself against the charge of incest with such cogency, passion and eloquence that the betting among the people was ten to one that he would be acquitted. But to the charge that he had used expressions showing that he doubted whether Elizabeth was Henry's child he made no reply and when he was handed a paper with a question written on it which he was forbidden to read aloud, he, knowing that nothing would prevent his judicial murder, proclaimed the contents in a loud voice—'that the King was not able to have relations with his wife: that he had no virtue or potency in him.' This, as Chapuis, the Spanish ambassador, reported to Charles V, infuriated Cromwell who was anxious not to have suspicion cast on Elizabeth's paternity, since Henry though now determined to have her technically bastardized in law was, comprehensibly, equally determined to insist that he was her father.

The fifth man who was charged with adultery with Anne was Mark Smeaton, who stands in a different category from the others. He was of no political significance, being not a 'gentleman' but 'of low degree'; from first to last—from whatever motive—he admitted the amour and died the terrible death of disembowelling, castration, hanging and quartering (the others were simply beheaded) without retracting it. When Anne heard that his last words on the scaffold were: 'Master, I pray you all pray for me, for I have deserved death,' she is reported to have said: 'Has he not then cleared me from the public shame he hath done me? I fear his soul will suffer for the false witness he hath borne.'

To reconstruct the story of Mark Smeaton and Anne at this distance of time, with all the key documents destroyed, is almost impossible. The sources that remain are, among official records, his indictment and the mention in the Privy Purse expenses of some forty grants to him of shirts, hose, shoes, buskins, boots and money in the three years before Elizabeth's birth*. There are ambassadorial dispatches; a Spanish *Chronicle of King Henry VIII*, which gives a detailed account of matters as they were known to Spanish merchants living at the time in London; a contemporary French life of Anne Boleyn which gives a strange and highly-coloured account, of which some portions can be checked against other narratives; a memorial to Cromwell from George Constantine (who was an eyewitness of the executions); letters of Cromwell and others; gossip and popular ballads, such as Cavendish's metrical account of Smeaton's parentage:

* The Privy Purse accounts (Add. Mss. 20,030) are from 17 November 1529 to the end of December 1532. They thus stop about nine months before the birth of Elizabeth. The accounts for these three years were preserved by coming into the hands of Sir Orlando Bridgeman in 1634. Although at present other accounts are missing, they may yet of course be discovered.

My father a carpenter and laboured with his hand,
  With the sweat of his face he purchased his living,
For small was his rent and much less was his land:
My mother in cottage used daily spinning.

and other occasional references.*

To some extent, the sources may be used to check each other to arrive at as much 'certainty' as can be found for most events of the time. One can say for example, that undoubtedly Smeaton was the first to be arrested, since Constantine, Chapuis, Cromwell, Bulkeley, the Spanish chronicle and two French accounts all agree on the point. And, where they can be compared, the statements of Cromwell, Constantine and the Chronicler (between whom there can have been no collusion) support each other so well that the *Chronicle* substantially may be relied on.

As far as it can be pieced together from the sources

---

* Bishop Burnet, in his *History of the Reformation* (published in 1679, the year the 'Popish Plot' scare was at its height, as a piece of Protestant propaganda), says that he took great pains in searching for documents which might throw some light on the proceedings and managed to find an entry in the private note-book of Sir John Spelman, one of Smeaton's judges, which ran: 'As for the evidence of the matter, it was discovered by Lady Wingfield, who had been a servant to the Queen and becoming suddenly infirm before her death, did swear this matter to one of her . . .' Here the page containing the vital information is torn off and with it the other notes of the judge have disappeared.

There is nothing in Burnet's character or methods which makes it improbable that he himself destroyed both this and any other document which he found embarrassing to his cause. The Lady Wingfield story is uncorroborated, as Cromwell, in his letter to Gardiner, names no one in particular, saying merely that Anne's servants could not hide 'the Queen's abomination' any longer. Burnet's avowed purpose is to exonerate, as far as possible, Anne as the patroness of Protestantism and his alleged 'Wingfield fragment' enables him to contend that the main evidence against her and her lovers was hearsay evidence of an oath of a dead woman.

that have survived the destruction of the main documents, the story runs thus.

Mark Smeaton, who was in Anne's service while she was still only Henry's mistress, was sent for one morning when she lay in bed 'in her lodging above the King's' when they were staying at Winchester. She wished him to play that her ladies might dance.

He was young and very handsome and as she watched him she set her heart on having him for her lover. Since he himself would not take advantage of her obvious interest, she took into her confidence an old waiting-woman named Margaret, who lay at night in the ante-chamber of her room, between it and the gallery where, within hearing, the rest of Anne's ladies slept.

In this antechamber there was a cupboard where sweetmeats, candied fruits and preserves were kept. Here, one night, Margaret concealed Smeaton. When all was quiet Anne called out: 'Margaret, bring me a little marmalade' and the waiting-woman, leading Smeaton by the hand, said: 'Here is the marmalade, my lady.' Then Anne, so that the ladies in the gallery could hear—as they had heard but not understood the rest of the exchange—called out: 'Go along; go to bed.'

Smeaton continued so much in the Queen's favour that she gave him considerable gifts, which he spent on dress, jewels and horses. In time he became overbearing and insolent, after the manner of favourites, and quarrelled with some of the courtiers, in particular Sir Thomas Percy, the brother of the Earl of Northumberland.

Anne, on hearing of this, sent for Percy and ordered him to make up his quarrel with Mark. Percy, though forced to obey, continued to bear such a grudge that he went to Cromwell, told him of the favour Anne was showing to Smeaton and pointed out that the musician could not have acquired by fair means all the money he was in the habit of spending.

This was exactly what Cromwell needed. He asked Percy secretly to watch his enemy, with the result that, on April 29, 1536, Percy was able to report that he had seen Smeaton, early in the morning, coming out of Anne's apartments.

That particular meeting between Anne and Smeaton in the palace at Greenwich was too well-authenticated for it to be denied and Anne's account of it ran: 'Upon Saturday before May Day I found him standing in the round window in my Chamber of Presence and I asked why he was so sad and he answered and said it was no matter and then I said: "You may not look to have me speak to you as I should to a nobleman, because you be an inferior person." "No, no, madam, a look sufficeth me and thus fare you well." '

She also said that this was the only time she had spoken to him since the occasion when she sent for him to play the virginals in her bedroom at Winchester.

It will be noticed that Anne's explanation of Smeaton's sadness was that he was hopelessly in love with her. Smeaton's later explanation, probably under torture, was that Noreys and Bryerton were his rivals. These statements give the particular complexion to the affair that each speaker wanted—Anne of being innocent but accused of adultery by a love-crazed menial, Smeaton of deserving mercy by giving the names of two people whom Cromwell wished to remove. But, if the words were actually spoken—and the scene seems to me vividly true—there is surely a third possible interpretation. Smeaton must have been aware of the climate of the court, where it was quite well known that Henry had tired of Anne and was paying his attentions to Jane Seymour. The whole atmosphere was one of impending disaster and in less than three weeks, as it happened, both Smeaton and Anne would be dead. What was more natural than that he should make a desperate attempt to leave while there was still time and, in coming to say farewell, give Anne a warning to which, because he was a mere musician outside politics, she would pay no heed? Not only will the words bear this construction, but the situation seems to demand it.

In any case, Smeaton later that morning left the Court and, on his way back to London, he was arrested and taken to a house in Stepney where next day he was interrogated by Cromwell himself. Constantine wrote: 'I cannot tell how he was examined, but upon May Day in the morning he was in the Tower. The truth is he confessed it, but yet the saying was that he was first grievously racked, which I could never know of a truth.' The Chronicler says that the torture was by a knotted cord being tightened round his head. Another account is that he was induced to sign the deposition which incriminated himself and Anne as well as Noreys and Bryerton, not by torture but by the implied promise of Sir William Fitzwilliam, Lord High Admiral, who, seeing his hesitation and terror, said: 'Subscribe, Mark, and you will see what will come of it.'

The only thing certain is that, for whatever reason, Smeaton never denied his relations with Anne and the other four never admitted them. 'No one,' said Sir Edward Baynton, who was given the task of searching for evidence, 'will accuse her, but alonely Mark, of any actual thing.' And, as we have seen, when all hope of his life being spared (if he ever had such hope) was gone, Smeaton persisted, at the edge of death, in his plea of guilty. And as he had pleaded guilty at his trial, no examination was necessary there. The indictment referred to a single act of adultery, on April 26, 1534, to which Anne had 'procured and incited' him a fortnight earlier. That April, seven months after Elizabeth's birth, Anne had told Henry she was pregnant, which, as she had to admit in September, was untrue.

[iv] Anne and Henry

Anne's acquaintance with the King had begun soon after 1521, when she returned from France (where she had been brought up at Court), to find that her younger sister, Mary, was Henry's mistress. The King soon transferred his affections to the vital, sophisticated newcomer into the Boleyn household, who, however, knowing the rumours that he intended to divorce his wife, Catherine of Aragon and marry someone who could give him an heir, is said to have kept him at arm's length as the surest way to inflame his passion and ultimately gain the Crown. Whatever their relationship may have been Anne was a power to be reckoned with in the late 'twenties though she did not become Henry's officially recognized mistress till the autumn of 1532, when the death of the old Archbishop of Canterbury, William Warham, who had stubbornly resisted all the King's attempts to divorce Catherine, meant the disappearance of the last obstacle to eventual marriage. The new Archbishop, Cranmer, could be counted on to do whatever Henry ordered and was, indeed, appointed only for that purpose.

Anne accompanied Henry to France as his *maîtresse-en-titre* in the October of 1533, returning to England in mid-November. In December, Cranmer arrived from Italy to be made Archbishop of Canterbury and, according to accepted belief, Henry and Anne were secretly married on January 25, 1533.*

When Elizabeth was born, Henry made no attempt to hide his disappointment and irritation at the sex of the child; and within six months, he had tired of Anne and was beginning to show interest in Jane Seymour.

It was at this point—the April of 1534—that Smeaton was said to have committed adultery with Anne and that Anne told Henry she was pregnant. The news, false though it was, had the effect of making the King show her once more some consideration and courtesy— which abruptly stopped when she had to confess that she was mistaken. In the February of 1535, Henry was considering divorcing her and only refrained because it was pointed out to him that, if he did, he would have to return to Catherine of Aragon. He would not be able to make a third marriage with Jane Seymour while two discarded wives were still alive.

---

* Jane Dormer, however, said that the marriage was only four months before Elizabeth's birth on September 7 and that, for that reason, Camden had concealed the date—as, indeed, he has. The January 25 date, which is now assumed by all historians, rests on Cranmer's statement in a letter which he wrote on June 17, that it took place 'about St Paul's day' (one may be permitted to suppose that had Cranmer known the true state of Anne's pregnancy, he would have ante-dated it), combined with the Duke of Norfolk's information to Catherine of Aragon on April 9, that the King had been married to Anne Boleyn for over two months.

During 1535 Anne realized that her only hope of holding Henry was by bearing him a son. She was pregnant again in the September of that year, but miscarried in January 1536, on the very day of Catherine of Aragon's funeral. Henry had no pity. He went to her bedside and told her that he now saw God would not give him a son and that when she recovered, he would speak to her. She knew then, since Catherine's death had removed the obstacle to Henry's marriage with Jane Seymour, that her divorce was merely a matter of time, though it is improbable that she foresaw her death.

After Anne's arrest and trial, three months later, as Rochford's proclamation of Henry's impotence and Smeaton's admission of his own adultery, made it impossible for the King to bastardize Elizabeth by adducing proof that Elizabeth was not his child, another excuse had to be found. Though this simple solution was apparently originally under consideration and the Spanish Ambassador actually heard a rumour that it was being used, Henry for mere pride's sake, would not hear of it. He insisted that Elizabeth should be recognized as his daughter, yet be proclaimed a bastard. The only method of doing this was to find that his marriage to Anne had been invalid from the beginning. Cranmer, who had originally declared it valid, immediately obeyed Henry and two days before Anne's execution solemnly declared it null on the grounds that a man could not properly marry the sister of his mistress. And as Mary Boleyn had admittedly been the King's mistress before his marriage to Anne, Anne could never have been truly Henry's wife.

In all this tangle of lying, chicanery and lust, anything like certainty is even more impossible than usual in history. And there is, to complicate the matter still further, the implication in Friedmann's verdict, with which few who have studied the matter will disagree: 'While I am strongly of the opinion that the indictments were drawn up at random and that there was no trustworthy evidence to sustain the specific charges, I am by no means convinced that Anne did not commit offences quite as grave as most of those of which she was accused. She may have been guilty of crimes which it did not suit the convenience of the government to divulge. At the trial some hints to this effect were thrown out and, though proof was not adduced, they were likely enough to have been true.'

It must also be added that, as a statute had been passed in the autumn of 1534 making treasonable any statement capable of being interpreted as a slander upon the King's issue, it had become, in fact, impossible to accuse Anne officially of misconduct before Elizabeth's birth, however much evidence there might have been.

We may, therefore, sum up the matter by saying that, though 'proof' is lacking, Mary Tudor's tenaciously-held belief and open assertion that Elizabeth was the daughter of Anne Boleyn and Mark Smeaton equally cannot be 'disproved' and that what facts are known support rather than rebut the claim.

3

THE POISONING OF
KING JAMES I

On March 5, 1625, King James I, who was at his
favourite country residence at Theobalds, was taken
ill of a tertian ague. It was not considered serious and
on March 11, he was well enough to sign and dispatch
a safe-conduct for the Conde de Gondomar, the former
Spanish ambassador who was then in Spain, to return
to England. Among other things, Gondomar was bound
to bring an adverse report on the Duke of Buckingham's
recent conduct in Spain, and the gossip at court was
that he was returning at the King's invitation 'to put a
flea in the Duke's ear.' Nobody, least of all Buckingham,
doubted that the Spaniard's coming would 'mean the
Duke's discredit.' The day after the safe-conduct was
signed, James was sufficiently strong to contemplate
being moved to Hampton Court and Buckingham, who
had been going to and fro between Theobalds and his
own residence, Wallingford House, in London, arranged
with his mother to send to Dunmow for a special plaster
made by a doctor there.

The Countess of Buckingham applied the plaster to
the King's wrists, in defiance of protests from his
doctors; and James grew rapidly worse. As soon as the
plasters were taken off and normal medical treatment
restored, the King once more improved. On March 21

the plasters were again applied and the King grew so very much worse that one of the doctors, Craig, used such strong language that he was ordered to leave Court, while another, Hayes, was called out of bed to take the plasters off.

Buckingham then had prepared by his own servant, Baker, a special julep which he took to James with his own hand. James drank twice but refused the third time. This was on March 22.

On March 23, all hope of the King's life was abandoned. The Bishop in attendance on him told him that his end was near and the next day he received Holy Communion in company with all his attendants except Buckingham, who excused himself on the grounds that he had stomach-ache.

On March 27, James died. Immediately afterwards a paper was brought to the doctors to sign 'that the ingredients of the julep and the plasters were safe,' but, even knowing what the displeasure of the now all-powerful Buckingham meant, they refused. (Their conduct in this matter was sworn on oath by the physicians themselves before a select Committee in 1627.)

When, in 1626, Buckingham was impeached by the House of Commons, the thirteenth article of the charge referred to these events, though the specific accusation of poison was avoided. To save the Duke, Charles I dissolved Parliament.

For over two hundred years after James's death, the theory that Buckingham poisoned him was never seriously called in question. The only problem which engaged the attention of historians was whether or not King Charles I was privy to it; or at least implicated in the sense in which the accusation was put by Milton: 'To omit other evidences, he that would not suffer a Duke that was accused of it to come to his trial must needs have been guilty of it himself.'

When, in 1653, Bulstrode Whitelock was the English ambassador to Sweden, he found Queen Christina interested in the subject. She asked him the details of the matter. He had been in the 1626 Parliament, and as a lawyer and the son of a judge, had weighed the evidence carefully. After his recital of the facts of the case, Queen Christina replied: 'Certainly he was poisoned' and thus endorsed the general contemporary verdict.

The reversal of this verdict to such an extent that the mere asking of the question nowadays is held 'unworthy of a serious historian' is due entirely to S. R. Gardiner, who is accepted, without any attempt at verification, by academic historians. In the fifth volume of his *History of England*, published in 1883, Gardiner assumes that the medical evidence for poisoning is worthless. This conclusion, he bases on a pamphlet written in 1862 and published in Calcutta by Dr Norman Chevers, Principal of the Calcutta Medical College: *Did James the First of England die from the Effects of Poison?* Gardiner dismisses the weighty circumstantial evidence as worthless because, he says: 'the only ground for supposing it to have any value is cut away once it is understood that Buckingham had no object in poisoning the King.' As Gardiner's own reconstruction of that background is one of his own more obvious inaccuracies and his treatment of the event is marked by his usual technique of suppressing awkward facts, his opinion is of little value. It has not even the merit of making a real case;

for Dr Chevers admits that the administration of the julep, even if it were quite harmless, would aggravate the illness and pronounces that 'nothing could have been less appropriate,' citing as an example 'a Superintendent's Surgeon in the Bengal Medical Service who died in 1856, whose fatal attack was excited by a draught of beer shortly followed by one of milk.' Thus, if the question is put in the form: 'Did Buckingham kill the King?' ignoring the question of poison, Dr Chevers's pamphlet is not on S. R. Gardiner's side.

One may therefore pose the question as an unsolved historical mystery.

[i] The Evidence of Poison

It is most convenient to start with the strongest argument against actual poison, which is that James's health was so ruined by his long debaucheries that his end was only to be expected. This is substantially the argument of Dr Chevers in his pamphlet.

The Venetian Envoy, reporting to the Doge two years before the King's death wrote: 'Good principles and feelings are extinguished in him. He loves nothing but himself, his own convenience and his pleasures. He distrusts everyone, suffers from extreme weakness of mind and is tyrannized over by constant fear of death.'

The French ambassador, the Comte de Tillières, who left England after a five-year's stay in the June of 1624, noticed that Buckingham, whose early ascendancy over James was due to simple and overpowering sexual infatuation, was now keeping that control by additionally encouraging all James's vices. In the

October of 1623, he wrote: 'The weightiest and most urgent affairs cannot drive this King to devote to them even a day, nay, an hour, or to interrupt his gratifications. These consist of his betaking himself to a remote spot where, out of the sight of men, he leads a filthy and scandalous life and gives himself up to drinking and other vices. .... It appears as if the more his strength wastes away, the more these infamous passions increase and, passing from the body over to the mind, assume a double power.' And in the February of 1624, he noted: 'Buckingham confirms him in everything and hopes that, the more he abandons himself to all pleasures and to drunkenness, the weaker will be his understanding and spirit and so much the easier will he be able to rule when the other ties of connection are dissolved.'

These are objective reports of foreigners, intent only on getting the exact truth to report to their masters; and their evidence, as far as Buckingham is concerned is confirmed by the Duke's own letters to James. In the July of 1624 for instance, when he feared the rivalry of one of his younger relatives in James's affections, he writes that he wonders 'whether you love me now better than at the time I shall never forget at Farnham, where the bed's head could not be found between the master and his dog.' And in the October of 1624, he wrote (adding, comprehensibly, at the end: 'I pray you burn this letter') of a man who had come to him with a remedy for James's indispositions: 'I confess so long as he concealed the means he wrought by, I despised all he said; but when he told me that which he hath given Your Sovereignship to preserve you from all sickness ever hereafter was extracted out of a turd, I admired the fellow and for these reasons: that, being a stranger to you yet he had found out the kind you are come of and your natural affections and appetite and so, like a skilful man, hath given you natural physic.'

The picture emerges of an ageing debauchee wrecking —and encouraged to wreck—his health with excesses, under the superintendence of the Favourite. Of the King's chronic drunkenness, there can be no doubt. It was reported and commented on from all quarters and, as early as 1621, de Tillières had mentioned that he was 'lost in pleasures and buried for the greater part of his time in wine.' When, after death, James's body was opened by his physicians they found 'his heart of an extraordinary bigness, all his vitals sound, as also his head, which was very full of brains; but his blood was wonderfully tainted with melancholy; and the corruption thereof supposed the cause of his death.'

The tertian ague, attacking such a constitution, was obviously serious though it need not have been mortal; and the most significant fact seems to be that James was recovering until the application of the plasters to his wrists and stomach.

Such plasters were the commonplace of contemporary treatment for the disease. 'The pulses of the wrists' and the pit of the stomach, were the spots chosen for the application of these external remedies. One such prescription was a compound of 'frankincense, cinnabar, camphire, wood-soot, turpentine and the like'; another 'used by the vulgar' was a hard-boiled egg split and applied hot to the wrists. Bruised spiders and tobacco were one recipe and another a combination of yarrow and rue with the buds of honey-suckle, bramble and elder. A favourite concoction was mouse-ear with vinegar and salt, wall-pepper, shepherd's purse, sundew and vervain.

The composition of the plaster applied to James is not ascertainable, but one of the royal physicians, Dr George Eglisham, about a week after the King's death, was on a visit with Sir Matthew Lister to the Earl of Warwick's house in Essex, near Dr Remington, the Dunmow doctor (who was Warwick's physician) who had supplied the plaster. They sent for Remington to ascertain from him the ingredients. After Remington had told them that it was 'mithridate spread upon leather', Sir Matthew Lister produced a piece of the actual plaster which had been applied to the King. On examining it, Dr Remington was much surprised and offered to take an oath that it was not the same that he had sent to the Duke.

Dr Eglisham, a Scot, had been James's physician since 1616. His hobby was writing poetry and he seems to have been both eccentric and extreme in his views. Shortly after his appointment as Royal physician he had undertaken to prove in his *Duellum Poeticum* that the King's boyhood tutor, George Buchanan, had been guilty of 'impiety towards God, perfidy to his Prince and tyranny to the Muses.' His famous pamphlet accusing Buckingham of murder, *Prodromus Vindictae*, was published in 1626, the year after James's death, and must be treated with considerable reserve, if only because immediately after its publication, Eglisham fled to the Continent to escape punishment by the infuriated Duke.

To treat the pamphlet with reserve, however, is not entirely to dismiss it as evidence. For one thing, all the doctors agreed with Eglisham at least to the extent that, knowing the danger of offending Buckingham, they all refused to certify that the plaster was harmless. For another, it was published at a time when its reference to living persons could be verified and—had not Charles dissolved the 1626 Parliament to save Buckingham from having to answer for his conduct—would have been either verified or disproved at the Bar of the House of Lords. And, finally, much of the material in it is corroborated by other writers.

Eglisham's account runs: 'The King being sick of a tertian ague, which in the spring was of itself never found deadly, the Duke took this opportunity, when all the doctors of physic were at dinner, upon the Monday before the King died, to offer to him a white powder to take, the which he a long time refused; but, overcome with his flattering importunity, at length took it in wine and immediately became worse and worse, falling into many swoonings and pains and violent fluxes of the belly, so tormented that His Majesty cried out aloud of this white powder: "Would to God I had never taken it! It will cost me my life."

'In like manner also the Countess of Buckingham, my Lord of Buckingham's mother, upon the Friday, the physicians being also absent and at dinner and not made acquainted with her doings, applied a plaister to the King's heart and breast; whereupon he grew faint and short-breathed and in a great agony. Some of the physicians, after dinner returning to see the King, by the offensive smell of the plaister perceived something to be about him hurtful to him and searched what it should be and found it out and exclaimed that the King was poisoned. The Duke of Buckingham entering commanded the physicians out of the room, caused one of them to be committed prisoner to his own chamber and another to be removed from Court; quarrelled with others of the King's servants in his sick Majesty's own presence so far that he offered to draw his sword against them in His Majesty's sight. And Buckingham's mother, kneeling down before His Majesty, cried out with a brazen face: "Justice, justice, sir, I demand justice of Your Majesty!" His Majesty asked her for what? "For that which their lives are no ways sufficient to satisfy; for saying that my son and I have poisoned your Majesty." "Poisoned me?" said he: with that, turning himself, swooned; and she was removed.'

That some such scene took place, there can hardly be any doubt. Meade, in one of his letters to Sir Martin Stuteville informed him that the Countess of Buckingham 'would needs make trial of some receipt she had approved but, being without the privity of the physicians, occasioned so much discontent in Dr Craig that he uttered some plain speeches, for which he was commanded out of Court, the Duke himself (as some say) complaining to the sick King of the word he spake.'

Dr Craig, who was as definite as Dr Eglisham in his belief that Buckingham had poisoned the King, was one of a family of physicians and lawyers. His father, Dr John Craig, an M.D. of both Basle and Oxford, had been James's physician before he became King of England and, in that capacity, had accompanied him south. His uncle, Sir Lewis Craig, had been an advocate, trained in France and, as Lord Wrightslands, had become a Scottish Judge. His grandfather, Sir Thomas Craig, had been famous as an advocate, a justice and an authority on feudal law. With this background and training, Dr Craig was likely to be more accustomed

to weighing evidence and less predisposed to emo-
tionalism than Dr Eglisham. His nephew by marriage,
the father of Bishop Burnet, who was in London at the
time of the King's death 'did very much suspect an
ill-practice in the matter,' having heard his uncle's
evidence.

James Howell, the writer, traveller and diplomatist
who was later to become historiographer-royal to
Charles II, was at Theobalds at the time of James's
death and, in a letter to his father, mentioned the complaints of the doctors that a plaister had been applied to
the 'outside of the King's stomach' by the Countess of
Buckingham, though he committed no other comments
to paper. Bishop Goodman, who was also there, though
he entirely exculpates Buckingham, evidently believed
that there was foul play. He writes: 'I have no good
opinion of his death, yet I was the last man that did
him homage in the extremity of his sickness.' Arthur
Wilson, the contemporary historian of the reign records:
'The King, that was very much impatient in his health,
was patient in his sickness and death. Whether he had
received anything that extorted his agueish fits into a
fever, which might the sooner stupify the spirits and
hasten his end, cannot be asserted; but the Countess of
Buckingham had been tampering with him in the
absence of the doctors and had given him a medicine
to drink and laid a plaister on his side of which the
King much complained and they did rather exasperate
his distemper than allay it and these things were
admitted by the insinuating persuasions of the Duke
her son, who told the King they were approved medicines
and would do him much good. And though the Duke
often strove to purge himself for this application, as

having received both medicine and plaister from Dr Remington, at Dunmow, in Essex, who had often cured agues and such distempers with the same; yet they were arguments of a complicated kind, not easy to unfold, considering that whatsoever he may have received from the doctor in the country, he might apply to the King what he pleased in the Court.'

What Buckingham's unofficial efforts to 'purge himself' of suspicion were, we have no record; but we have his official answer made to the charges of the Commons in 1626. This defence, which is printed in full in the appendix, seems to me to confirm rather than allay suspicion. It explains almost too well those facts of the situation which were incontrovertible. His uncorroborated dove-tailing is a little too perfect. And, it must be reiterated, Charles's dissolution of Parliament to prevent it being tested by evidence is a strong argument against its accuracy.

According to the Duke, it was the King who asked for the plaister and the posset-drink, as it had done Buckingham good in a recent attack of ague. Buckingham, though he admitted the efficacy of the remedies, delayed sending for them and only did so after the King had personally ordered the Duke's servant, Baker, to go and fetch them from Dunmow. Buckingham asked James not to use them until after they had been tested on one of the Gentlemen of the Bedchamber and two children in the town who had ague and then to use them only on the advice of his doctors. The King promised to do so.

At this point, Buckingham left Theobalds and went up to London, returning to the King's bedside at the precise moment when James was drinking the

'posset-drink' which had, in the meantime, arrived.
James asked Buckingham to administer it to him, which
he did, after the doctors and various other people in the
room had tasted it. Later, when the King grew worse,
Buckingham heard the rumour that 'his physic had
done the King hurt' and had been given without advice.
He told the King of this and James answered: 'They
are worse than devils that say it.'

It will be seen by this account that the points which
are too well attested by witnesses to be denied are
admitted but explained in another sense. The medicine
from Dunmow was fetched by Buckingham's servant,
Baker—but it was the King, not the Duke, who sent
him for it. Buckingham administered the fatal draught
to James—but the King was already on the point of
drinking it when the Duke arrived back from London.
Buckingham complained to the King of the slanders—
but the King's answer was favourable to the Duke.

Secondly, Buckingham goes out of his way to assert
that other people tasted the drink, including some of
the physicians—which cannot be made to tally with the
physicians' own evidence before the Select Committee.
Thirdly, no mention at all is made of the administration
of the 'plaisters' which, as Buckingham admitted that
he had recommended them, were also ultimately his
responsibility.

Sir William Sanderson, another contemporary historian who was also the Earl of Holland's secretary,
records that 'what Buckingham gave James to drink
was a posset-drink of milk and ale, hartshorn and mari-
gold flowers, ingredients harmless and ordinary'—
though, as Dr Chevers has pointed out, any drink at
that point would much aggravate the illness and nothing

could have been less appropriate. (And, on his analogy of the beer and milk drunk by the surgeon in Bengal, it would have been by itself sufficient to cause death.)

There were, of course, more scurrilous tales than these, written by the anti-Royalist pamphleteers. One will suffice—that by Sir Anthony Weldon who, originally Clerk of the Green Cloth at James's court, had been dismissed for satirizing the Scots and who eventually joined the Parliamentarian side in the Civil War. He published in 1650 his *Court and Character of King James I* which contained much unreliable gossip and is rightly regarded by historians, even when they use it, with the maximum of suspicion. He writes: 'He (James) now goes to his last hunting journey (I mean the last of the year, as well as of his life, which he ever ended in Lent) and was seized of an ordinary Tertian Ague, which at that season, according to the proverb, was Physic for a King; but it proved not so to him and, poor King, what was but physic to any other was made mortal to him. Yet not the ague, as himself confessed to a servant of his who cried: "Courage, Sir, this is but a small fit; the next will be none at all"; at which he most earnestly looked and said: "Ah, it is not the ague afflicteth me, but the black plaister and powder given me and laid to my stomach."

'And in truth the plaister so tormented him that he was glad to have it pulled off and with it the skin also. Nor was it fair dealing, if he had fair play (which he himself suspected, often saying to Montgomery whom he trusted above all men in his sickness: "For God's sake, look I have fair play!") to bring in an Emprick to apply any medicines whilst those physicians appointed to attend him were at dinner. Nor could any but

E   129

Buckingham answer it with less than his life at that present, as he had the next Parliament had it not been dissolved upon the very questioning him for the King's death and all those that prosecuted him utterly disgraced and banished the Court.

'Buckingham coming into the King's chamber even when he was at the point of death and an honest servant of the King's crying: "Ah, my Lord, you have undone us all, his poor servants, although you are so well provided you need not care": at which Buckingham kicked at him, who caught his foot and made his head come first to the ground, where Buckingham presently rising runs to the dying King's bedside and cried: "Justice, Sir, I am abused by your servant"; at which the poor King mournfully fixed his eyes on him as one who would have said: "Not wrongfully," yet without speech or sense.'

The credibility of Weldon is neither more nor less than that of any other 'gossip' (such as Creevey, for instance, at the Hanoverian court) but the passage about Montgomery—who, as Earl of Pembroke, lived till 1650 and, at least in his earlier days at court as one of James's favourites was well-known to Weldon—has about it the ring of authenticity.

To sum the matter up, it is incontrovertible that the fifty-nine-year-old King was in an enfeebled state of health but that no one expected the tertian ague to be mortal; that certain unknown remedies were applied in defiance of the doctors by Buckingham and his mother; that the King grew worse after each application and that hope for his life was finally abandoned after Buckingham had administered a 'posset-drink'; that two doctors, Eglisham and Craig, publicly accused

Buckingham of causing the King's death; that all the doctors, even though under pressure, refused to certify the remedies harmless; that the charge against the Duke though in a necessarily modified form, was formally made by the House of Commons and that a proper investigation was officially stopped by the Crown (which Buckingham controlled); that informed contemporary opinion was overwhelmingly in favour of Buckingham's guilt and even those who, like Bishop Goodman, considered the Duke personally innocent, were suspicious of foul play on somebody's part. Against this must be set the fact that, after the autopsy, the King's death was 'supposed' to be due to the 'corruption' of his blood which was 'wonderfully tainted with melancholy'—a vague diagnosis which, at this distance of time, is difficult to appraise correctly and which may or may not be compatible with poison.

On all this S. R. Gardiner comments: 'The evidence is worthless in itself and the only ground for supposing it to have any value is cut away when once it is understood that Buckingham had no object in poisoning the King.'

It is therefore necessary to examine the position of Buckingham at the time of James's death.

[ii] The Position of Buckingham in 1625

The keystone of James's foreign policy was a Spanish alliance, of which one of the terms was intended to be Spanish aid to restore the Palatinate to his son-in-law, who had been driven out of it. To cement the alliance, Prince Charles was to marry the Infanta Maria, sister of the King of Spain. Gondomar, the powerful Spanish ambassador in London, returned to Spain in 1622 to superintend negotiations in Madrid, with the English ambassador there, the Earl of Bristol.

In 1623 Prince Charles, accompanied by Buckingham, went to Madrid to woo the Infanta in person. Their visit was kept secret as long as possible from the House of Commons in England, who, having inherited all the Elizabethan prejudices, were violently anti-Spanish and did not understand that, in the new century, it was France under Richelieu, not Spain, which was the strongest European power and, as such, the 'natural' enemy of England (whose policy, then as always, was in self-interest to allow no nation to have the hegemony of Europe).

There were seven chief actors in the comedy of 'the Spanish Match.' On the English side, the thirty-year-old Buckingham, the twenty-two-year-old Charles and the forty-three-year-old Bristol, the one competent English statesman of the age. On the Spanish side were the seventeen-year-old King, Philip IV, who cared for nothing but hunting and was entirely dominated by his minister, the thirty-six-year-old Olivares; the Infanta, who was sixteen—and Gondomar, who at fifty-six, was one of the ablest diplomatists in Europe, and whose return to Spain Olivares had insisted on as being the only man capable of coping with Bristol.

Bristol, who believed that the restoration of the Palatinate should be settled diplomatically on its merits and confused neither by concessions to the 'religious' prejudices of Protestant mobs in England nor by secret clauses in a marriage treaty, had been at the outset opposed to the idea of the marriage, but he had loyally endeavoured to carry out his master's instructions. On the one hand, he denied the right of Spain to interfere with the religious policy of England; on the other, he had bargained for the best possible terms from Spain which, he considered, would be safer as an ally than as an enemy of England.

The arrival of Buckingham and Charles undid all his work. They stayed in Madrid exactly twenty-five weeks. During that time, Buckingham contrived to offend everyone, from the populace who said that they would 'rather put the Infanta headlong into a well than into his hands,' to Olivares himself, who eventually told him in public that he looked upon his friendship as a thing of no importance. He wrecked all Bristol's diplomacy, destroyed any hope of continuance of good relations between England and Spain and at the same time injured the chances of a satisfactory settlement of the Palatinate question.

The result was due to his unique combination of political incompetence with personal arrogance. In England, though he was the all-powerful Favourite and transmitted the King's orders, the details and routine of government had remained in the hands of trained officials. His own contribution had been limited to interference, from personal motives, which lessened the efficiency of the administration or increased the confusion of the King's celebrated 'statecraft.' On his arrival in Madrid, because of his position with James, he took the control of negotiations out of Bristol's hands, and when Bristol was forced to remonstrate with him, treated him 'worse than a dog.' Never before having tried his own unaided hand at diplomacy and having no aptitude for it, Buckingham was consistently out-manœuvred by Olivares.

As with his lack of political acumen, so with his personal behaviour. In England he was so accustomed to treat King, nobles and commoners alike as if they were his servants that he did not realize how this behaviour would affect those trained in the rigid etiquette of the Spanish Court. It was not so much that he was intentionally rude as that he had no idea of any other code of manners.

The Spaniards, accordingly, were further antagonized by seeing Buckingham lounging in a dressing-gown and without breeches at the Prince's table, turning his back on him in public and shouting at him in questionable nicknames. They were disgusted when Buckingham leant rudely forward to stare at the Infanta, and again when he created a scene, followed by a fit of sulking, because Bristol was invited to share a carriage with the King and Prince. He offended the clergy by bringing one of the official theological conferences to a sudden and unconventional end by 'expressing his contempt for the Friars by unseemly gesticulations' and then throwing his hat on the ground and jumping on it. The courtiers were insulted by his indiscriminate amours, which were such a source of scandal that he was even suspected of an attempt on Olivares's wife and his illness in the summer attributed to a disease caught from a 'notorious stew' who was sent, heavily veiled, to impersonate her. Bristol was eventually moved to write home to James: 'I must, for the discharge of my conscience and duty, without descending to particulars, let Your Majesty truly know that suspicions and distastes betwixt them all here and my Lord of Buckingham cannot be at greater height.' His judgment was confirmed by the fact that, on the pillar set up in a field by the Escurial to commemorate the visit, the Spaniards omitted the name of Buckingham 'as if he had been none of the company.' But Bristol's honesty in the report meant his ruin.

From the moment he arrived back in England, in the autumn of 1623, Buckingham had only one object—to revenge his wounded vanity by precipitating a war against Spain. In this policy, he had the support of the House of Commons and, indeed, of the country in which, for the first and last time, he became a popular figure—the Prince's good angel who had foiled the wicked Spaniards. He had, too, the enthusiastic support of Charles, of whom, in Spain he had made a lasting conquest.

This friendship, indeed, was the most significant fact to emerge from the Spanish journey. No historian has sufficiently recognized (what is abundantly evident from contemporary records as well as Domestic and Foreign —especially Venetian—State Papers) that until 1623 Buckingham and Charles were on exceedingly bad terms. All biographers of Buckingham have put their reconciliation years before it in fact took place and consequently do not allow for the full meaning of Madrid, where, if Charles fell in love with anyone it was not with the Infanta but with Buckingham.

I do not of course mean that Charles had physical relations with him. The Favourite's known relation with the Prince's father would preclude that, even if there had been no other reason. But Charles became far more deeply attached to Buckingham than even James had ever been and from the return from Spain until Buckingham's murder five years later, that passionate affection never wavered. From 1624, Buckingham could control Charles as he could never, even in the first flush of James's infatuation, control James. And from that time, from the point of view of power as well as from the point of view of amorous convenience, Buckingham must have preferred Charles to James as King. What is more, he did not conceal it. To a French visitor, James confided that he did not know what devil had entered into Buckingham since he returned from Spain and the Duke himself did not trouble to hide from the King his knowledge that his conduct was causing the comment that 'I am suspected to look more to the rising sun than to my maker.'

It is this which gives a certain poignancy to James's letter to Buckingham in the Christmas of 1624: 'I cannot content myself without sending you this billet, praying God that I may have a joyful and comfortable meeting with you and that we may make at this Christenmas a new marriage, ever to be kept hereafter; For, God so love me, as I desire only to live in this world for your sake, and that I had rather live banished in any part of the earth with you, than live a sorrowful widow-life without you. And so God bless you, my sweet child and wife, and grant that ye may ever be a comfort to your dear dad and husband, James R.'*

But, throughout 1624, Buckingham, though secure in the support of the Prince and the Parliament and the people, knew, that as long as James retained any kind of control of policy, there was the danger that he might learn the truth about Spain and that, in the circumstances, such a revelation might destroy him. Though he seemed all-powerful, he was under no illusions on

---

* Generations of historians have incorrectly ascribed this letter as written to Charles!

what, ultimately, his power depended. As he had supplanted Somerset as the Royal minion, so he might be supplanted by some younger and more attractive rival. And if the political and personal motives coincided in James's mind, he was lost.

It so happened that he had a potential rival, a young kinsman of his own, Arthur Brett.

Just before the journey to Spain, at the end of 1622, James and Buckingham had had a violent quarrel over Arthur Brett, who had been made a Gentleman of the Bedchamber and had very obviously attracted the King's notice. It was a matter not only of court gossip but was serious enough to engage the attention of the Venetian ambassador, who reported it to the Doge with the comment: 'Some who observed the fate of the earlier favourite, Somerset, think that His Majesty's favour is like the summer sky from which, when quite serene, a thunderbolt sometimes falls unexpectedly.'

Before he left for Spain, Buckingham thought it advisable to take all possible precautions against being supplanted in his absence and Brett was accordingly knighted and sent abroad. Young Monson (who, five years earlier had been thought of as a rival favourite and washed his face hopefully each morning in 'posset-curd') was similarly exiled. In the March of 1624, however, when Brett returned from his Continental travels, he was welcomed by James with such affection that Buckingham dared not let James out of his sight. Unfortunately, that May, various strains had become too much for him. He collapsed and for three weeks was dangerously ill of—as one reported it—'a fever, the jaundice and I know not what else; so that, beside other physic, he hath been let blood thrice at least; yet the world thinks he is more sick in mind than in body and that he declines apace,' and when he was well enough to return to Court—in mid-June—he found Brett in such favour that the Venetian ambassador at least believed that the Duke's absence had been due not so much to illness as to James's changed affection.

Certainly Brett's hold had become strong enough for Buckingham to need a month to break it, but by the middle of July he had managed it and Brett was told to keep away from James.

The young man, however, was of an impatient disposition and shortly afterwards, when James was hunting in Waltham Forest, he ignored the ban, rode up to him and laid hands on the bridle of his horse. This was all that Buckingham needed. Brett was sent to the Fleet prison and, though he was released after about six weeks, he was forbidden thereafter to come within ten miles of London or the Court.

But, for the remaining eight months of James's life, Buckingham could not free himself from the fear of the emergence of another rival, or even of Brett's own return.

It is against this background that one must consider the more direct threat to Buckingham's position which would have materialized on the arrival of authentic and incontrovertible news from Spain.

The first danger was the return of Bristol, who arrived in England at the same time as Brett—in the March of 1624. Buckingham's influence was still sufficient to ensure that he was not allowed to see James. His attempt to have the ambassador sent to the Tower was, indeed, unsuccessful, but James, though he promised Bristol he would not condemn him unheard, ordered him for the moment to confine himself to his own manor of Sherborne. When Bristol, though forced to obey, asked that the Commons should make the fullest possible investigation of his conduct, he was told that the end of the session was near and Buckingham tried to bribe him to silence by offering to forget the past. Bristol replied: 'In the matter of my fidelity and loyalty towards His Majesty, the Prince and my country, I hope I shall never see that come into compromise, but shall rather lose my life and fortunes than to admit the least stain to remain on me or mine in that kind.' But he was never allowed to see James again.

Gondomar's confessor, Lafuente, who was also dispatched from Spain to inform James of the truth of things, called for different measures. Buckingham had him waylaid near Amiens and all his papers stolen, so that when he was conducted to James's presence he had to admit that he had lost his credentials. Eventually he managed to get a private audience with the King and told him that it was Buckingham's conduct in Spain, of which he had been kept in ignorance, that had caused the present dangerous situation. James was interested enough to want to know more and two days later, Inojosa, the Viceroy of Navarre, who had been sent to England to support the attempt to save the Spanish alliance, completed the story. If the King refused to go to war with Spain, he said, Buckingham intended to force him to abdicate in favour of Prince Charles.

With Parliament and the country in its present mood, this was quite a feasible plan. James was to be kept amused with hunting and other pastimes at Theobalds until the time was ripe. The King was frightened. In his

youth in Scotland men whom he had loved as much as
he loved Buckingham had conspired to hold him in
terror of his life. And there was nothing in the present
behaviour of the Prince and the Duke which made the
present story intrinsically improbable. James told
Inojosa to let him have the charges in writing and left
Theobalds immediately for the comparative safety of
Windsor Castle. On his way, he called at St James's
Palace where Buckingham was with Charles. As they
came out to welcome him, he burst into tears and cried:
'Steenie, Steenie, wilt thou kill me?'

Buckingham naturally protested his innocence; the
Privy Council, when it was summoned to investigate
Inojosa's charges, found they were too vague to be
sustained and, the Councillors swearing one by one
that they had never heard a treasonable word pass
Buckingham's lips, they found the Duke not guilty.
Inojosa was asked to leave the country and forbidden
to have another interview with the King.

There is no reason whatever to suppose that his story
was untrue; and that the abdication was not seriously
planned.

As soon as Inojosa reached Spain, it was determined
to send Gondomar himself once more to England. This
news was, as even S. R. Gardiner admits, 'very terrible'
to Buckingham. With Gondomar's arrival, the Duke
was likely to be ruined for ever. He could survive the
imputations of Inojosa and discredit Lafuente; he could
prevent Bristol from ever seeing the King; but Gondomar
was invulnerable. Nothing could keep him from James's
presence and nothing could bribe him to hold his tongue.
Even with Parliament, he could shatter Buckingham's
temporary popularity by merely revealing the secret

clauses of the Spanish treaty and, being what he was, he was not likely to hesitate, should it become necessary.

At all costs Gondomar must not come; and yet there was no possible way of preventing him. But there was a way of preventing him seeing James. On March 11, 1625, a courier started for Spain with a safe-conduct for Gondomar, and a personal letter from James. On March 12, James was well enough to consider moving from Theobalds to Hampton Court. On March 23, after the treatment of the plasters and the julep, all hope of his life was abandoned and on March 27, he was dead.

Gardiner's suggestion that 'Buckingham had no object in poisoning the King' seems to me, in these circumstances, the exact reverse of the truth and should be dismissed as completely as his other and cognate theory that James's interest in Buckingham was 'paternal' is now repudiated by all historians.

Buckingham's blood-guiltiness stands, in fact, exactly where it did before Gardiner wrote, when the verdict of 'Guilty,' which accords with the known facts, was accepted without demur.

APPENDIX

Article XIII of the charge against Buckingham at his impeachment.

Whereas special care and order hath been taken by the laws of the realm to restrain and prevent the unskilful administration of physic whereby the health and life of man be much endangered; and whereas most especially the royal persons of Kings of the realm (in whom we, their loyal subjects, humbly challenge a great interest), are and always have been esteemed by us so sacred that nothing ought to be prepared for them or administered unto them in the way of physic or diet in the times of their sickness without the consent and direction of some of their sworn physicians, apothecaries or surgeons; and the boldness of such (how near soever to them in place and favour) who have forgotten their duties so far as to presume to offer anything unto them beyond their experience, hath always been ranked in the high offences and misdemeanours.

And whereas the sworn physicians of our late sovereign Lord King James, of blessed memory, attending on His Majesty in the month of March, in the 22nd year of his most glorious reign, in the times of his sickness, being in ague, did, in due and necessary care of and for the recovery of his health and preservation of his person, upon and after several mature consultations in that behalf had and holden at several times in the same month, resolve and give directions that nothing should be applied or given to His Highness by way of physic or diet during the said sickness but by and upon their general advice and consents and after good deliberations thereof first had more especially by their like care and upon like consultations did justly resolve and publicly give warning to and for all the gentlemen and other servants and officers of his late Majesty's bed-chamber that no meat or drink whatsoever should be given unto him for two or three hours next before the usual time of and for the coming of his fit in the said ague, nor during the continuance thereof, nor afterwards until his cold fit was past: the said Duke of Buckingham, being a sworn servant of his said late Majesty and in His Majesty's said bed-chamber, contrary to his duty

142

and the tender respects which he ought to have had for His Majesty's most sacred person and after the consultations, resolutions, directions and warnings aforesaid, did nevertheless, without any sufficient warrant in that behalf, unduly cause and procure certain plaisters and a certain drink or potion to be provided for the use of his said Majesty, without the direction and privity of his said late Majesty's physicians, not prepared by any of his sworn apothecaries or surgeons but compounded of several ingredients to them unknown; notwithstanding the same plaisters (or some plaister like thereunto) having been administered unto his said Majesty did produce such ill effects as that some of the said sworn physicians did altogether disallow thereof and utterly refuse to meddle any further with his said Majesty until these plaisters were removed as being hurtful and prejudicial to the health of His Majesty; yet, nevertheless, the same plaisters, as also a drink or potion, was provided by the said Duke, by colour of some insufficient and slight pretences, who did upon Monday, the 21st day of March in the 22nd year aforesaid, when His Majesty by the judgment of his said physicians was in the declination of his disease, cause and procure the said plaister to be applied to the breast and wrists of his said late Majesty.

And then also, at and in His Majesty's fit of the said ague, the said Monday and at several times within two hours before the coming of the said fit and before His Majesty's then cold fit was past, did deliver and cause to be delivered several quantities of the said drink or potion to His Majesty, who thereupon, at the same times within the seasons in that behalf prohibited by His Majesty's physicians, as aforesaid, did by the means and procurement of the said Duke drink and take divers quantities of the said drink or potion. After which said plaisters and drink or potion applied and given unto and taken and received by His Majesty, great distempers and divers ill symptoms appeared upon His Majesty insomuch that the physicians, finding His Majesty the next morning much worse in the estate of his health and holding consultations thereabout, did by joint consent send to the said Duke praying him not to adventure to minister to

His Majesty any more physic without their allowance and approbation.

And his said Majesty finding himself much diseased and affected with pain and sickness after his then fit when by the course of his disease he expected intermission and ease, did attribute the cause of his trouble unto the said plaister and drink which the said Duke had so given and caused to be administered unto him.

Which said adventurous act by a person obliged in duty and thankfulness done to the person of so great a King after the ill success of the like formerly administered, contrary to such directions as aforesaid and accompanied with so unhappy event to the great grief and discomfort of all His Majesty's subjects in general, is an offence and misdemeanour of so high a nature as may justly be called, and is by the said Commons deemed to be, an act of transcendant presumption and of dangerous consequence.

II. *The Duke of Buckingham's answer.*

To the Thirteenth Article of the charge, which is set forth in such an expression of words as might argue an extraordinary guiltiness in the Duke who by such infinite bonds of duty and thankfulness was obliged to be tender of the life and health of his most dread and dear sovereign and master, he maketh this clear and true answer:

That he did not apply nor procure the plaister or posset-drink, in the charge termed to be a potion, unto his late Majesty; nor was present when the same was first taken or applied; but the truth is this: that His Majesty, being sick of ague, took notice of the Duke's recovery of an ague not long before and asked him how he had recovered and what he found did him most good. The Duke gave him a particular answer thereto that one who was the Earl of Warwick's physician had ministered a plaister and a posset-drink to him and the chief thing that did him good was a vomit, which he wished the King had taken in the beginning of his sickness. The King was very desirous to have that plaister and posset-drink sent for; but the Duke delayed it; whereupon the King impatiently asked whether it was sent for or not. And, finding by the Duke's speeches he had not sent for it, his late Majesty sent J. Baker, the Duke's servant, and with his own mouth commanded him to go for it; whereupon the Duke besought His Majesty not to make use of it but by the advice of his own physicians, nor until it should be tried by James Palmer, of his bed-chamber, who was then sick of an ague and upon two children in the town; which the King said he would do.

In this resolution, the Duke left His Majesty and went to London and in the meantime the plaister and posset-drink was brought and applied by his late Majesty's own command. At the Duke's return, His Majesty was taking the posset-drink and the King then commanded the Duke to give it him; which he did in the presence of some of the King's physicians, they then no ways seeming to dislike it, the same drink being first tasted by some of them and divers others in the King's bed-chamber; and he thinks this was the second time the King took it.

Afterwards, when the King grew somewhat worse than before, the Duke heard a rumour as if his physic had done the King hurt and that the Duke had administered that physic to him without advice. The Duke acquainted the King therewith, to whom the King, with much discontent, answered thus: 'They are worse than devils that say it.' So far from the truth it was; which now notwithstanding, as it seemeth, is taken up by some and with much confidence affirmed.

And here the Duke humbly prayeth all your lordships not only to consider the truth of this answer, but also to commiserate the sad thought which this article had revived in him.

4

THE EXECUTIONER OF
KING CHARLES I

On Tuesday, January 30, 1649, a bitterly cold day even
for winter, with the Thames frozen over and a grey sky
threatening snow, King Charles I was executed on a
scaffold outside the Banqueting House in Whitehall—
'at his own front door barbarously murthered.' He was
kept waiting for death for four hours, from ten o'clock
till two. This, however, was not intentional cruelty on
the part of his enemies; it was because no executioner
could be found. And the secret of the identity of the
two who eventually volunteered as headsman and
assistant was so well kept that it is a mystery still.

Both men were dressed alike in close-fitting woollen
frocks, like those worn by butchers or sailors, with
frieze trunk breeches. Their faces were impenetrably
masked by large vizards and the disguise was completed
by wigs and false beards. The executioner's wig, 'a grey
grizzled periwig,' hung very low: his assistant had a
black wig and beard and affected a large flapped black
hat, looped up in front.

Early that morning Colonel Daniel Axtell had sent
his brother, Elisha, with a guard of soldiers to Wapping
to escort the common hangman, Brandon, with his
tackle, to Whitehall; but there seems little doubt that
when he got there, Brandon, despite bribes and threats,

refused to do the deed. He was put under arrest at Whitehall until the execution was over and immediately afterwards sent home with five pounds in half-crowns as compensation.

A waterman named Abraham Smith narrated that 'as soon as that fatal blow was given' he was walking about Whitehall when a file of musketeers in charge of Brandon asked him where the official bargemen were. As there were none to be seen, they directed Brandon into Smith's boat.

'Going into the boat,' said Smith, 'he gave one of the soldiers a half-crown. Said the soldiers: "Waterman, away with him, Begone quickly"; but I, fearing the hangman had cut off the King's head, I trembled that he should come into my boat, but dared not examine him on shore for fear of the soldiers; so out I launched and having got a little way in the water, said I: "Who the devil have I got in my boat?"

'Says my fellow, says he: "Why?"

'I directed my speech to him saying: "Are you the hangman that cut off the King's head?"

' "No, as I am a sinner to God," saith he, "not I." He shook every joint of him. I knew not what to do. I rowed away a little further and fell to a new examination of him when I had got him a little further. "Tell me true," said I, "are you the hangman that cut off the King's head? I cannot carry you," said I.

' "No," saith he, "I was fetched with a troop of horse and I was kept a close prisoner at Whitehall, and truly I did not do it. I was kept a close prisoner all the while, but they had my instruments."

'I said I would sink the boat if he did not tell me true; but he denied it with several protestations.'

Less than six months after the execution Brandon died. In 1680, over thirty years later, Dr Thomas Tenison became Rector of St Martin's-in-the-Fields and his chaplain has left on record that, during his incumbency, he was sent for to pray by a dying man in a poor house in Gardner's Lane, Westminster. 'He made haste but found the man just expired. The people of the house told him that the man (whose name they never knew) had been very anxious to see him and to confess to him that he was the executioner of King Charles; that he was a trooper of Oliver's and, every man in the troop having refused to do that office, Oliver made them draw lots and, the lot falling upon him, he did the work in a mask, and that he immediately mixed in the crowd, hiding the mask; that he had never been easy in mind since. He had lived some time in their house, was poor and melancholy and much distressed for want of consolation from Dr Tenison.' If this story be true, it is, of course, conclusive evidence against the possibility of Brandon being the executioner. Yet, since the majority of historians, following S. R. Gardiner, incline to the belief that Brandon was the headsman, one more piece of evidence may be adduced.

In the June 19–26, 1649 issue of *The Kingdom's Weekly Intelligencer*, under the date of Saturday, June 23, occurs the following:

On Wednesday last, the hangman departed this life and on the Sunday before, a young man, a friend of his, coming to visit him asked him whether he was not troubled in conscience for cutting off the King's head. He replied, Yes, by reason that upon the time of his trial and at the denouncing of sentence against him, he had taken a vow and protestation wishing

149

God to perish his body and soul if ever he appeared
on the scaffold to do the act, or lift up his hand against
him; further acknowledging that he was no sooner
entered upon the scaffold but immediately he fell
a-trembling and hath ever since continued in the
same.

He likewise confessed that he had £30 for his pains
all paid him in half-crowns within an hour after the
blow was given, which money he gave his wife at
six o'clock that night and told her that it was the
dearest money ever he earned in his life. He was very
much disturbed in his sickness and lay raging and
swearing and still pointing at one thing or another,
which he conceived was visible before him.

A little before the death of the aforesaid Richard
Brandon he, being in some discourse with a neighbour
touching the executing of the King, said that even at
the very point of time when he was to give the blow
a great pain and ache took him about the neck
and hath since continued; and that he never slept
quietly in his mind, saying that he was afraid to walk
along the streets or go to his bed and sleep without
a candle burning.

The other fellow that was upon the scaffold, that
went in the name of his man, was one Ralph Jones
and ragman, who liveth in Rosemary Lane. And he
who now takes his place as executioner is one William
Loe, a dust carrier and cleaner of dunghills.

This account was taken word for word from a
pamphlet entitled *The Confession of Richard Brandon*, a
pseudo-Royalist satire, which was put about by the
Cromwellian government so that, by fixing the crime
on a dead man, they could divert suspicion from the

real executioners. Such a purpose was admitted. The publication was 'to the end that the world may be convinced of those calumnious speeches and erroneous suggestions which are daily spit from the mouth of Envy against divers persons of great worth and eminency by casting an odium upon them for the executing of the King; it being now made manifest that the aforesaid executioner was the only man that gave the fatal blow and the man that waited upon him was a rag-man living in Rosemary Lane.'

What, therefore, might have been taken—indeed, has been taken—as evidence that Brandon was the executioner turns out to be, when all the circumstances are considered, even stronger evidence that he was not. The newspaper item and the pamphlet from which it was copied prove only, if they can be held to prove anything, that the authorities were exceedingly anxious to conceal the real identities of the men on the scaffold.

Finally, there is the significant fact that when, in 1660, William Hulet was on trial on the charge of being the executioner, though his defence was that the dead Brandon was the real culprit, he dared not call as a witness the hangman's widow, Mary Brandon, although he had originally announced his intention of doing so.

Dismissing Brandon, despite S. R. Gardiner and Sir Sidney Lee (who in the article in the *Dictionary of National Biography* describes Brandon quite simply as 'the executioner of Charles I'), we must next examine the credentials of this William Hulet who was tried on the charge and found guilty—though not, as far as any record exists, executed—at the Restoration.

Hulet's own story was that he was a sergeant in Colonel Hewson's troop which was on duty in Whitehall on the day of execution; that he, with six or eight other sergeants from various regiments had in the morning been called together, sworn to secrecy and asked to volunteer as executioner; that he had refused and, because of it, had been kept a close prisoner in Whitehall till ten o'clock at night.

The name of Hulet as a suspect was first mentioned during the trial of Colonel Daniel Axtell who must have known the identity of the executioners. During the Commonwealth, Axtell had been promoted, sent to Ireland and eventually appointed Governor of Kilkenny. When, after the Restoration, he was indicted, one of the witnesses was Lieutenant-Colonel John Nelson, second-in-command of another regiment in Ireland.

'My Lords and gentlemen of the jury,' said Nelson, 'upon a discourse with the prisoner at the bar in Dublin five or six years since' (that is, in 1654 or 1655), 'upon the platform of that Castle, I desired to know of him who it was executed the King, thinking he might inform me. He was pleased to tell me this.

'Saith he: "The persons who were employed in that service, you know as well as I do."

' "Not I," said I. "I saw them in vizards but not their visage, as I know of."

' "Yes," saith he, "you do know them. It is true myself and others were employed in that affair in the ordering of the execution; but there were several persons came and offered themselves out of a kind of zeal to do the thing, but we did not think it proper to employ persons we did not know; but we made choice of a couple of stout persons."

' "Pray let me hear their names," said I.

'Said he: "It was Hulet and Walker." '

Axtell interrupted the witness: 'You named one man: I did not hear the other.'

'I named Hulet and Walker,' said Nelson, loudly.

'Was anybody by?' asked Axtell.

'No, sir,' Nelson admitted.

'Did I name anybody to you?'

'You named those two persons.'

'Certainly I must have invented them, then,' retorted Axtell, 'for I had no more knowledge of them than anybody here.'

'You told me,' said Nelson, 'that you were one of those who had the managing of the affair.'

The last remark is important in assessing Axtell's denial; for the reason the executioners were mentioned at all in his trial was merely to establish that, since he knew who they were, he must *ipso facto* have been one of the Colonels in charge of the final arrangements. As this fact was unchallenged, the matter of the executioners, as such, was irrelevant and Axtell's point in denying knowledge of the men's names was merely to avoid convicting himself out of his own mouth. So well was this understood that, when Hulet himself was brought to trial later the same day, Axtell, in spite of being asked, did not give evidence.

At Hulet's trial, Nelson repeated his evidence, with the additional information that Hulet was the assistant and Walker the headsman. He also asked that Colonel Pretty, then in Ireland, should be sent for to corroborate the evidence, for, though he refused to swear positively, his recollection was that Pretty also had named Hulet.

The first witness against Hulet was Richard Gittens, who claimed to have been a fellow sergeant with him in the same company for about thirteen years. Gittens said: 'A day or two before the King came to the scaffold, Colonel Hewson did give notice to the lieutenant that we should come to him, about thirty-eight of us, and he put us all to our oaths that we should say nothing of what they did. He swore us to the Book. After he had sworn us, he asked us if we would undertake to do such an act. If we would, we should have a hundred pounds down and preferment in the Army. We refused, every person. We thought Hulet did refuse. After all refused, it seems he did undertake to do the deed.

'When the King was brought on the scaffold, we were in Scotland Yard and they were upon the guard in the Banqueting Chamber. When they were there I laid down my arms and got into the Company. Captain Webb kept the guard with his halberd in his hand by the scaffold and I did bustle to come near to them. Then I returned back. Hulet, (as far as I can guess), when the King came on the scaffold for his execution and said: "Executioner, is the block fast?" fell upon his knees to ask him forgiveness. By his speech, I thought it was he.

'Captain Atkins said: "Who would not undertake to do this act?"

'I told him I would not do it for all the city of London.

' "No, nor I either, for all the world," saith Atkins. "You shall see Hulet quickly come to preferment." And immediately after he was made Captain-Lieutenant.'

'Was Hulet with his regiment that day?' asked the counsel.

'We could not see him with the regiment all that day,' replied Gittens. 'He was never absent at any time before.'

'Did you know his voice?'

'Yes, sir.'

'Did you mark the proportion of his body, or his habit—what disguise he was in?'

'He had a pair of frieze trunk breeches,' said Gittens, 'and a vizard, with a grey beard; and after that time Colonel Hewson called him "Father Greybeard" and most of the army besides. He cannot deny it.'

Hulet, however, denied everything. He denied that he and Gittens were sergeants in the same company; he denied that he was ever called 'Greybeard' and he denied that Gittens had been in a position to hear any voice on the scaffold. The questioning was swift.

'Where were you at the time when the act was done?' asked Hulet.

'Where was I?' said Gittens. 'By Captain Webb.'

'Where was he?'

'At the door of the Banqueting House.'

'Was you on the scaffold or no, sir?'

'I was on the scaffold end.'

'My Lord,' said Hulet to the judge, 'I desire you to consider what this person says. He was on guard in Scotland Yard and at the scaffold with Captain Webb!'

The topographical divergence, however impressive as a debating point, is by no means conclusive. What Gittens had said, it will be remembered, was that he was in Scotland Yard, went to the scaffold at the time of the execution and returned. At that time Scotland Yard was one of the three courts of Whitehall Palace and contained the Guardroom; and the end of the scaffold was at a little building annexed to the Banqueting House on the north side. Anyone today, merely by walking from Old Scotland Yard to the entrance of the United Services Museum, can make the experiment of

timing how long it would have taken Gittens (who, as
he was in Scotland Yard, was presumably in reserve,
not on duty) to get from the one place to the other.
Five minutes leaves a comfortable margin for going
there and back at a walking pace.

As for Hulet's denial that he and Gittens were in the
same regiment, it may be true that, *on that day*, they
were separated; but Hulet made no attempt to answer
the charge that they had been fellow-sergeants for
thirteen years (which could have been checked), in
which case Gittens's identification of a well-known
voice in the profound silence which fell on the crowd
when the King came on the scaffold would have been
easy enough.

Later evidence against Hulet from Captain Toogood
was more damning. 'I was in 1650, about September,
in Dublin Castle about some business with Colonel
Hewson,' he said. 'Captain Hulet came into the room
and talked with Colonel Hewson a little while. I observed
them very familiar and I asked Hewson what he was.
He told me he was his Captain-Lieutenant of horse. I
desired to know where he had got him. He said he had
made him so from a sergeant and a very mettled fellow
he was. It was he that did the King's business for him
upon the scaffold.

'In 1653,' continued Captain Toogod, 'there was a
disbanding of the army in Ireland. This gentleman was
then continued Captain-Lieutenant in Pretty's regiment.
I discoursed with Pretty concerning him and one part
of it, I remember, was about the King's death; and he
did tell me that he was assured by Colonel Hewson that
Hulet either cut off the King's head or held it up . . .

'About twelve months after, I came to live near the

prisoner in Ireland. Once I remember at one Mr
Smith's, at the White Horse in Carlow I met him there
and I asked him whether he was the man who cut off
the King's head or no.

'Saith he: "Why do you ask me this question?"'

'I told him I had heard so by Hewson and Pretty.
Upon that he said: "Well, what I did I will not be
ashamed of. If it were to do again, I would do it."'

'Once since that time, about half a year afterwards,
I was in the same place and there talking with him
about the King's death. He was telling me it was true
he was one of the two persons who were disguised upon
the scaffold. I desired to know what if the King had
refused to submit to the block.

'Saith he: "There were staples about the scaffold and
I had that about me that would have compelled me"
—or words to that effect. . . . I have observed in Ireland
that it hath been generally reported that he was either
the man that cut off the King's head, or that held it up;
as I have said before. And I have heard them sometimes
call him "Grandsire Greybeard." ' '

There was further evidence on both sides, but none
of it satisfactory. The story told by a soldier that, in a
tavern over several pints of wine, Hulet though not
admitting that he did it, yet justified the execution was
cancelled out by a 'stranger'* Hulet called to testify
on his behalf who did not take the oath and merely
reported: 'I was with my master in the company of
Brandon the hangman and my master asked Brandon
whether he cut off the King's head or no. He confessed
in my presence that he was the man that did cut off the
King's head.' The evidence of a spectator in the crowd

* So entered in the report of the trial; there is no clue to his identity.

that the executioner was of the same build as Hulet was hardly more valid than the uncorroborated affirmation of another that he once heard Brandon confess to the act. But the fatal weakness of Hulet's case was that he dared not call Mary Brandon, because she had already given evidence on oath before the Lord Mayor which ran counter to that of the witnesses for the defence.

In the evidence of a soldier named Stammers and Hulet's questioning of him, the possibilities are nicely balanced.

Stammers identified Hulet as Captain-Lieutenant of Colonel Hewson's troop in which Stammers served in Ireland. . . . 'When I had entered myself into that troop,' said the witness, 'I was a while in Dublin and I was commanded by the prisoner at the bar, I and the rest, to march to a place named Lutterel's-town, about five miles beyond Dublin. The prisoner at the bar came thither to us two days after. Then, being in his chamber, he sent for me. I went up and sat down. He examined where I had served. I told him I did formerly belong to the Lord of Inchiquin. He asked if I was ever in the King's army.* With that he walks about the room two or three turns. Saith he: "I was the man that beheaded King Charles and for doing it I had a hundred pounds," saying, "I was a sergeant at that time." '

---

* Murrough O'Brien, first Earl of Inchiquin, President of Munster, was a Royalist who temporarily submitted to Parliament because they had command of the seas and therefore controlled the supplies Inchiquin needed for the people of Munster. As soon as he had got the supplies, he gradually made himself master of the south of Ireland; fortified the southern ports against Parliament and openly declared for Charles I once more in 1648. After the King's execution, he fought against Cromwell as long as he could and in 1650 crossed to France. Hulet's question to Stammers is thus quite a natural one, and may, indeed, be taken as confirming the authenticity of the conversation.

'I desire to ask him a question,' said Hulet, 'I confess —what is your name?'

'Stammers,' said the counsel. 'His name is Stammers.'

'Such a one was under my command,' said Hulet. Then, turning to the witness, he said: 'I think I have not seen you these eight years. I desire to know when these words were spoken and the place.'

'In Lutterel's-town in your own chamber, nine or ten years ago.'

'It is about eight years since I left that command,' said Hulet. 'Who was by at the time?'

'Nobody.'

'Tis strange. How long had you been in the troop before?'

'I was in Dublin about a fortnight,' said Stammers. 'Then you sent for me and I came to Lutterel's-town. The first time that I came to the troop was at Dublin and then you came to me with two orders from Hewson; and then you did pretend you were the brother of one, Mr Chambers; and then we went and quartered in Lutterel's-town.'

'My Lord,' protested Hulet to the judge, 'his examination in Ireland and this doth not agree. You did deny this before Baldwin, a trooper. I desire his examination may be read.'

That examination was therefore read and, according to the note in the report of the trial, 'agreed with the testimony now given.'

'I desire that he may mention what man that was that I sent for him,' said Hulet.

'I cannot tell what man,' said Stammers.

'My Lord, I desire that servant may be either named or produced.'

'I cannot remember the man,' said Stammers. 'It was seven years ago.'

Hulet's version of the matter was that, at a tavern in Gorran, between Cullen and Munster, he and others were drinking, when the discussion turned on the execution of the King.

'Saith Stammers: "I did hear that you were one of the persons for that purpose."

'Said I: "They that say so do me wrong."

'Saith he: "It is no matter if you were so, for it was a just act."

'Said I: "Whether it was or no, I have nothing to do to justify it."

'He said: "As I hope to be saved, I would have done it." '

Between accusation and counter-accusation, the reader may judge, but it seems to me that, taking into consideration not only this but the rest of the evidence, the balance tips against Hulet. And the jury who listened to it all, 'after a more than ordinary time of consultation' decided in that sense. He was pronounced 'Guilty.' On the other hand, as no record of his execution exists, it may have been felt that the identification was not altogether conclusive.

About ten weeks after the trial, two petitions from him and a letter to the Speaker were reported to the House of Commons. Nothing further is known. Hulet slips unnoticed out of history. But he could have been the man who died twenty or so years later, asking for the Rector of St Martin's-in-the-Fields to come and ease his conscience.

If Hulet was the headsman, who was the assistant? It will be remembered that Lieutenant-Colonel John

Nelson, who first mentioned Hulet's name in the trials, said that Colonel Daniel Axtell named the second man as Walker. Henry Walker was the most famous and popular journalist of the time. Originally an apprentice to an ironmonger in the City, he went to Cambridge in 1639; was ordained, and was almost immediately suspended for his fanatical views. On the eve of the Civil War, he was imprisoned for writing scurrilous but lively libels under the names of Members of Parliament. He then tried to sell himself to the Court by publishing an apostrophe to the King.

> *... Charles, all Europe's splendour,*
> *Thine enemies' terror and true faith's defender*

in which he prayed:

> *That God which graced thee with a Royal Crown,*
> *Crown thee with grace, thy honours with renown!*

Finding no answering enthusiasm from the Palace, he joined in the Parliamentary army, and, a deadly enemy of the King, became the intimate friend of Cromwell, Hugh Peters and William Hewson. When the war was over, he set up in journalism and edited *Perfect Occurrences*, which became the official newspaper of the Army and the mouthpiece of Cromwell.

A week after the King's execution, Walker was concerned to deny in his paper the rumour that the executioner was a certain Colonel Fox and later he dealt with another *canard* on the subject: 'Some have lately laid an imputation on Captain Edward Frodsham that he was the King's headsman. But the contrary is attested by those in whose company he was. And, indeed, the report is ridiculous.' It is significant, also, that *Perfect Occurrences* made no reference to Brandon's death or suggested that he had been the executioner.

Henry Walker by his position and his contacts with the managers of the execution, almost certainly knew who the mysterious men were, though there is no reason to suppose that either he himself or his brother William* was one of them. The name of Walker appears only in Lieutenant-Colonel Nelson's evidence and was neither repeated nor in any way followed up. It is possible that an incident in his career as a professional journalist explains the mention of him.

In the first few months after the execution of the King, Parliament's official astrologer, William Lilly, and Cromwell's secretary, Robert Spavin, collaborated in the lucrative side-line of supplying forged passports to Royalists, some of which they managed to sell for as much as £50 apiece. The passports were all under Cromwell's hand and seal, obligingly supplied by Spavin, and they were distributed by Lilly whose eminence in fortune-telling had given him an immense clientele. When the matter eventually came to Cromwell's knowledge, he sent a full account of it to Henry Walker with the curt note: 'Mr Walker. Print this verbatim in your *Occurrences* for satisfying people how they and the Army have been abused.' Walker duly printed it (in June, 1649) and this exposure may account for the rumour that he was the executioner. Between 1649 and 1660 there was ample time for a

* William Walker was secretary to Major-General Lambert, a mathematician, the recipient, in 1681, of the honorary freedom of the Cutlers Company of Hallamshire (which suggests that the apprenticeship of Henry to an ironmonger was of the nature of a son going into the family business and would explain his subsequent appearance at Cambridge), was left undisturbed at the Restoration and was honourably buried in the parish church of Sheffield.

slander-campaign; and neither Spavin nor Lilly was scrupulous in denigration.

Lilly, however, left on record in print a curious story implicating another man, equally unlikely, the 'Cornet Joyce' who is known in popular history for his forcible abduction of Charles I from the Parliamentarians at Holmby House.

'The next Sunday but one after Charles I was beheaded,' wrote Lilly, 'Robert Spavin, secretary to Lieutenant-General Cromwell, invited himself to dine with me and brought several others along with him. Their discourse all the dinner time was only who it was that beheaded the King. One said it was the common hangman; another, Hugh Peters; others also were nominated but none concluded.

'Robert Spavin, so soon as dinner was done, took me by the hand and led me to the south window. Saith he: "These are all mistaken. They have not named the man who did the act. It was Lieutenant-Colonel Joyce. I was in the room when he fitted himself up for the work; stood behind him when he did it; when done, went in again with him. There is no man knows this but my master Cromwell, Commissary Ireton and myself." '

Quite apart from the intrinsic improbability of Joyce being the executioner or of Spavin standing behind him on the scaffold, no one is likely to credit any story told by William Lilly which has no independent confirmation. In this case, the business relationship of Spavin and Lilly makes it doubly untrustworthy; and the fact that Joyce was shortly afterwards cashiered and imprisoned for his opposition to Cromwell supplies a motive for Spavin's attempt to slander him.

In considering the identity of the assistant, we have

some small clues which are absent in the case of the executioner. One is the man's behaviour; another is his dress. When he held up the head of the King and everyone was waiting for the conventional shout: 'Behold the head of a traitor,' he said nothing at all. If any were disposed to think that this strange silence betokened sympathy with the victim, they were rapidly disabused by another solecism. He threw the head down on the scaffold with such force that the still-warm cheek was bruised. And in his dress he had, as we have noticed, a certain panache—a black hat 'cocked up,' not the unobtrusive cap of the executioner.

From such slender evidence it would, indeed, be impossible to draw any valid conclusions were it not that they all fit one who has persistently then and since been suspected—Cromwell's trusted Army Chaplain, Hugh Peters. He was the one man whose voice everyone would know—which would account for his silence. He was particularly venomous in his sadistic hatred of the King and had, on the morning of the execution, suggested—and superintended—addition to the scaffold of four staples to which hooks and pulleys were attached to drag the King like a beast to slaughter should the executioners think it necessary. And his florid exhibitionism which made him a power in the pulpit, was such that, in the days when Charles was a prisoner, he would ride in a coach before him with his own attendant escort.

The character of Peters in relation to the King may be epitomized in the incident of the sermon he tried to preach to him on the eve of his death. The text he had chosen was: 'All the Kings of the nations, even all of them, lie in glory, every one in his own house. But thou art cast out of thy grave like an abominable branch, and as the raiment of those that are slain, thrust through with the sword, that go down to the stones of the pit as a carcass trodden under foot.' 'This I did intend to insist and preach upon before the poor wretch,' said Peters, 'and the poor wretch would not hear me.'

Burnet's description of Peters as 'a sort of enthusiastic buffoon (though a very vicious man) that had been of great use to Cromwell and had been outrageous in pressing the King's death with the cruelty and rudeness of an inquisitor,' expresses the general judgment of the times, and is borne out by what is known of him. It was indeed his ordinary reputation that made him, at the time, an obvious suspect.

From the trials of the regicides, two points about Peters emerge. He was seen both before and after the execution. Richard Nunnelly, the door-keeper of the Committee for the Army, who went in with Cromwell to Whitehall after the morning session of the Commissioners at Westminster, saw and spoke to Peters in the Banqueting House as he was making the final arrangements for the scaffold. When the execution was over, he saw him again. 'I saw the vizards going into a chamber there,' Nunnelly said; 'about an hour afterwards there comes Hugh Peters in his black cloak and broad hat out of that chamber, (as I take it) with the hangman.'

There is nothing suspicious about these movements of Peters. On the contrary, they were, it might be argued, the natural things for him to do. It might be expected that he would examine the staples which, at his suggestion, had been driven into the scaffold; and it was equally probable that he, in common with others

of the Army, would be in conversation with the headsman and with Brandon, after the deed was done. Nor
was there any reason why he should not acknowledge
them. His actions on the day of execution itself would,
in view of his known attitude to the King and his proved
part in bringing him to trial and death, have no effect
on the inevitable sentence to be passed on him. He was
not on trial, as Hulet had been, for being an actual
participant in the execution.

It is when we find him desperately trying to establish
an alibi and denying that he was at Whitehall at all on
the day of the execution that our suspicions are aroused.
To prove that he was not there was obviously important
to him; but, in trying to prove it and failing, he went
far to confirm the suspicion that he was not only there,
but there in an important capacity.

The witness on whom he relied was his servant,
Cornelius Glover, who, alone of all the witnesses, did
not take the oath. Glover was twenty-one at the time
of the execution and just 'up from the country.' As his
personality emerges clearly from the report, it is worth
giving the evidence in full.

The Lord Chief Baron started the questioning:
'Where do you dwell?'

'In Paul's Churchyard,' said Glover.

'What is your quality of life?'

Peters answered for him: 'A servant of the King's.'

'I am not asking you, Mr Peters,' said the judge.

'I belong to the Post House,' said Glover.

'Pray hear him speak,' Peters urged.

'What would you have him asked?'

'Whether I was out of my bedchamber that day the
King suffered.'

'What do you say to that?' said Lord Chief Baron.

'I was come to Mr Peters a little before that time to live with him as his servant,' said Glover. 'It fell out on that day he was ill in his chamber. The soldiers in St James's House were all gone away. I had a desire to go to see the meeting where they were at Whitehall. Saith he: "Thou seemest to have a great desire to go and look about thee. It is very sad, but if you will go, you may." I did go over the Park.'

'What time?' asked the counsel.

'About noon.'

'What hour?'

'I do not know. I did not stay there. The soldiers and the people filled the place and I went back again to the chamber. I came back again within the matter of an hour's time.'

'Was the King dead before you came back?'

'They said he was not. When I went home he asked me what was doing. I told him there was a great crowd I could not come near. I stayed there an hour and then I went out again and still there was a crowd and I came back again and Mr Peters was in his chamber then.'

'Was he in bed or up?'

'I do not remember.'

'How old were you then?'

'I am not above thirty-two or thirty-three.'

'Was Mr Peters sick?'

'Yes, he was melancholy sick as he used to be.'

That ended the cross-examination. Everything depended on the truth of Glover's assertion that he returned to Peters (who had apartments in St James's Palace) and then went out again. The King was executed at two o'clock. The headsman and his assistant were not found finally till about one o'clock. Peters was seen by Nunnelly leaving Whitehall 'about an hour' after the death of the King. Thus allowing a quarter of an hour to walk across the Park from the garden of St James's to the Banqueting House, Peters could have left his apartments at quarter to one and been back at quarter past three. This is to take the reckoning at its longest, for the time between the finding of the executioners and the execution could have been less than an hour.

This time is fixed by the fact that, once the two men had been procured, the warrant empowering them to act was signed by Colonel Hacker, after some discussion in Ireton's room in Whitehall, and then 'immediately' after the King was led to the scaffold. It could, therefore, have been as late as half-past one. And, at the other end of the period, if Peters did in fact come out of the room with Brandon and if the waterman's independent evidence of Brandon's coming to his boat 'as soon as the fatal blow was struck' be correct, Nunnelly's 'about an hour' would be nearer half an hour, at the outside. Thus the crucial time for Peters's alibi is from 1.15 to 2.30. And it is precisely this time which is covered by his servant's aimless return. According to his own account, Glover got back about one o'clock and stayed with Peters till two o'clock. The story seems a little too good to be true.

After the counsel had finished with Glover, the Lord Chief Baron asked him: 'Did you desire to go out or did he send you?' which seems a reasonably clear indication that the mind of the Bench was working on these lines.

'I did desire to go,' said Glover, 'being newly come to London.'

'This gentleman,' said the judge to the jury, 'though not upon oath is examined and it is only to one particular, nothing at all to the main proofs.'

It was at that point that Peters revealed his motive. 'I bring him only,' he said, 'to vindicate myself from the aspersion of being on the scaffold.'

'They did not lay the weight of their evidence on that,' the Lord Chief Baron reminded him. And, indeed, except in Peters's own mind, it had nothing to do with the charges against him in which it was not even mentioned. What he was accused of was 'compassing and imagining the death of the King' and, in particular, as the Solicitor-General put it, that 'there are five places where he did consult about the King's death—at Windsor, at Ware, in Coleman Street, in the Painted Chamber and in Bradshaw's house and four witnesses to prove this; there are two witnesses to his comparison of the King to Barabbas . . . proof that he called the day of His Majesty's trial a glorious day, resembling the judging of the world by the saints. He prays for this (the King's death) in the Painted Chamber, preaches for it at Whitehall, St James's Chapel, St Sepulchre's. What man could more contrive the death of the King than this miserable priest hath done?'

But what he was anxious to defend himself against was 'the aspersion of being on the scaffold.' And, in trying to extricate himself by Glover from the charge which was never formally made in Court, he has (or so it seems to me) finally confirmed for posterity the suspicion that he was Hulet's assistant, who dared not let his voice be heard and who threw down the severed head of the King with wanton violence.

5

THE INNOCENCE OF
SIR JOHN FENWICK

*Dear Life, I always told you from the beginning what
would be the end of it. That you will find true. Get leave,
if possible to come to me, but I doubt it must be from the
King. He will answer now 'that I am in the hands of
Parliament'; so he will refuse to meddle; and when they
have condemned me by their Act, I expect all barbarity to
be used to me. This may be the last, for aught I know,
you may have from me. My circumstances alter so often.
God bless you and preserve you and reward you here and
hereafter for your love and kindness to me and remember
your poor unfortunate husband who loved you to his last.*

So runs one of Sir John Fenwick's letters to his wife,
written from Newgate while the Commons were
debating the Bill of Attainder condemning him to
death for High Treason in 1696. It had been impossible
for the Crown to find more than one witness against
him and as this precluded trying him by the ordinary
processes of law, King William III ordered him to be
disposed of by Act of Attainder. The Bill, which the
Tories fought tenaciously in both Houses as com-
promising the elementary principles of justice, passed
the Commons by 189 to 156 and the Lords by only 66
to 60.

Of the various charges against Fenwick, the only one

relevant to an enquiry about his innocence is that which charged him with conspiring to assassinate William III. That Sir John remained an open and avowed Jacobite, refusing to break his oath to the exiled James II when William usurped the English throne, no one, least of all himself, denied. He was thus technically guilty of 'adhering to the King's enemies,' which was High Treason if William were considered the rightful King. Fenwick, with thousands of others, did not so consider him, and, on the scaffold itself, proclaimed: 'I pray God to bless my true and lawful sovereign, King James, the Queen and the Prince of Wales and restore him and his posterity to the Throne again, for the peace and prosperity of this nation; which is impossible to prosper till the government is settled on a right foot.'

The situation, in fact, was an undecided and revolutionary one, in which 'treason' was a word of no meaning, except in the sense of Harington's couplet:

Treason doth never prosper: what's the reason?
For if it prosper none dare call it treason.

Since Fenwick's side did not prosper, his unswerving loyalty to his King could be termed 'treason,' and, in so far as he was guilty in that sense, the accusation was a tribute to his honour. Dying, he could say with truth: 'My religion taught me my loyalty, which I bless God is untainted; and I have ever endeavoured in the station wherein I have been placed, to the utmost of my power to support the crown of England in the true and lineal course of descent, without interruption.'

Assassination, however, was a different matter. That he was in any way implicated in the so-called 'Assassination Plot' he vehemently denied; and no one with any knowledge of his character is likely to doubt his word.

A year or two ago, Mr. J. A. K. Ferns, who had heard some of my broadcasts on historical mysteries, was kind enough to write to me to tell me that, at the end of 1951, he presented to the British Museum a collection of Fenwick papers including a collection of forty letters written by Fenwick, when he was a close prisoner in Newgate, to his wife, Lady Mary, and smuggled out by his lawyer, Christopher Dighton. 'I do not know how the papers came into the possession of our family,' Mr Ferns wrote, 'but I think a thorough investigation may prove Sir John not guilty.'

These letters, from one of which my opening quotation is taken, do indeed afford final psychological proof of Fenwick's innocence, were any needed. They complete the known picture of him as a man to whom the idea of a cowardly assassination would have been utterly impossible. They also reveal his realism and his under-standing of the forces against him. For example, to his wife's hope that the Lords might throw out the Bill even if the Commons passed it, he writes: 'My dear life and soul, I beg you not to grieve for me. It is impossible to save my life or honour either, now; for they will say I am a liar and with that infamy I shall die. . . . I have no hopes of the Lords, for if they will not pass it, they will bring the mob to cry for "Justice!" and the Commons will give no money till I am executed. It is for that that I prepare. All my trouble is that they will be so barbarous as never to let you see me more and that is insupportable to me.'

This new Fenwick correspondence is, I believe, being published in full and must eventually be considered by

historians in relation to the other known documents of
the time. But the Fenwick that emerges from it is the
same loyal, intrepid, intelligent man of the Border
whom we know from history—a man whose panache
would have made him at home in the company of the
Three Musketeers, to which rare company he, in
temperament, properly belongs.

[i] Sir John Fenwick

Sir John Fenwick was born, as far as can be ascertained,
in 1645, the year of Naseby. He was a Northumbrian
of some substance, married to Lady Mary Howard,
sister of the Earl of Carlisle. He went soldiering when
quite young, was a Colonel of the Foot at thirty
and Major-General at forty-three. He was M.P. for
Northumberland from 1677 at intervals till 1685.
Fanatically devoted to the Stuarts, he opposed the
Exclusion Bill designed to debar James II from the
Throne and, when James eventually became King,
Fenwick took an active part against Monmouth who,
as a tool of William of Orange and the Whigs, made
armed rebellion against James. When William himself,
with the Dutch Armada, came against England in 1688
and successfully overthrew his royal uncle-father-in-law,
Fenwick supported James till the last and, in the days
of William and Mary's rule, so openly proclaimed his
continuing loyalty to the exiled King that William gave
orders to close Hyde Park against him and his friends
whose swaggering behaviour had caused one of the
paths there to be known as 'Jacobite Walk.' On one
occasion, when William and Mary were passing,

Fenwick so far allowed his principles to overcome his manners as to omit to raise his hat—a discourtesy which William never forgave.

During the impressionable years from five to fourteen, Fenwick had grown up under the usurpation of Oliver Cromwell. No loyalist then doubted that the King would come into his own again; nor, when similar forces to those which had killed Charles I drove his son, James II, into exile, did the loyalists doubt that the usurpation of William, too, would end with the King's return.

Because we know the outcome—that Charles II was restored but James II was not—it is never easy for us to enter into the situation as it was before the outcome was known. In this, as in so many other cases, the apparently futile game called 'the Ifs of History' is an essential element in understanding history. One of the main deformations in all thought about the past is the assumption that what did happen had to happen and that the attitude of men involved in an unresolved matter conforms with the judgment and perceptions of those wise after the event.

Even the casual reader today would never describe a man who in 1656 remained faithful to the exiled Charles II throughout the military usurpation of Oliver Cromwell a 'traitor,' whereas he is only too prone to apply the term to one who, forty years later, remained faithful to the exiled James II throughout the military usurpation of William of Orange. And the reason, possibly subconscious, is that the one usurpation was successful and the other was not. In so far as the differentiation is conscious, it is due to the Whig propaganda version of events which, equating success with legality, represents William's accession by right of conquest as more 'constitutional' than Oliver's.

Moreover, in 1696, as Mary was dead even William's pretended claim to the Throne as her husband was no longer admissible.* And William himself was prepared to recognize as his successor James II's son, the Prince of Wales who was in France with his father, provided that James would allow the boy to be educated as a Protestant. Though this proviso made certain—as presumably it was intended to—that James would refuse to consider the proposition, it at least revealed William's own attitude to a fluid situation.

The state of the country, at that time, bore witness to the Dutchman's rule. William had always hated the English but, in his megalomaniac warfare against France on his own behalf as Stadholder of Holland, he had seen their usefulness as a source of men and money; during his eight years on the English throne he had poured them out unstintingly. By 1696, beside the loss of lives, William was six million pounds in debt, the currency had depreciated to an extent unknown before or since, and the price of corn (which might be considered the equivalent of our modern cost-of-living index) had doubled. The resultant misery and unrest among the ordinary people made the climate of opinion propitious for a Stuart restoration. Even among the real rulers of the country—the multi-millionaire cabal

* Mary II's claim was not valid in her father's lifetime, whereas Mary I was indubitably Queen in her own right. Those who contend that after Mary II's death, William III was the rightful King of England, are logically forced to admit, *a fortiori*, that Philip I was the rightful King of England after Mary I's death. They are so far from doing this that very few but historians realize that the correct and official description of Mary I's reign after her marriage in 1554, is that of 'Philip and Mary,' whereas everyone knows the later 'William and Mary.'

which had financed William in his original attack on James—there was a reaction in James's favour. The very men who, when James was on the throne, had intrigued with William to unseat him—Shrewsbury, Churchill, Godolphin, Russell and the rest—were now intriguing with James to unseat William.

Taking all these circumstances into consideration, Sir John Fenwick's implication in the scheme for a Stuart restoration in 1696 was certainly not regarded by himself and cannot reasonably be regarded by anyone else as 'treason.' On the contrary Fenwick did only what was demanded of him by his original oath of allegiance to King James II, which he had kept when so many others had broken it.

So the Duke of Berwick, when he came secretly to England to organize the Stuart counter-attack, could note that 'there were two thousand horse ready to take the field to join the King [James II] on his arrival. Sir John Fenwick, a Major-General, was to take command of them.'

[ii] The Duke of Berwick's Mission

James FitzJames, Duke of Berwick, was twenty-six. He was the eldest son of James II by Arabella Churchill. He was already a hardened and acclaimed soldier when, at the age of seventeen, he had come to England and remained as his father's loved and trusted companion through the revolution of 1688. He went into exile with the King—the father, in fact, escaped to France disguised as the son's servant—and fought for him throughout the Irish campaigns from 1689 till 1691,

177

when James recalled him to France. He then joined
with the French armies in the Low Countries in the war
against William and earned and incurred William's
lasting hatred by one episode.

At the battle of Neerwinden, Berwick, in charge of
the two centre brigades, had carried the village and
driven the enemy beyond it, when he found his retreat
cut off. To regain his own lines, he took out his white
cockade in order to pass as an officer of the enemy.
Unfortunately his aide-de-camp was recognized by one
of Berwick's Churchill uncles, who was fighting for
William. He—as Berwick tells it—'suspected immediately that I might be there and, advancing to me,
made me his prisoner. After mutual salutations he told
me he must conduct me to the Prince of Orange. We
galloped a considerable time without meeting with him;
at last we found him at a great distance from the place
of action, in a bottom, where neither friends nor enemies
were to be seen.' William did not like that and the
meeting of the brothers-in-law was not, at least on
Berwick's side, cordial. 'The Prince made me a very
polite compliment, to which I only replied by a low
bow: after looking steadfastly at me for an instant, he
put on his hat and I mine; then he ordered me to be
carried to Lewe.'

William, contrary to the rules of war, continued to
hold Berwick. 'The Prince of Orange certainly had a
design of sending me prisoner to England where I
should have been closely confined in the Tower of
London, though that would have been contrary to all
the rules of war; for, though he pretended that I was
his subject and consequently a rebel, yet he had no
right to treat me as such, since I was not taken prisoner

in a territory that belonged to him. We were in the country of the King of Spain and I had the honour to serve as Lieutenant-General in the army of the Most Christian King [Louis XIV]: so that the Prince of Orange could be considered in no other light on that ground than as an auxiliary.'

Eventually Berwick was released in an exchange of prisoners and for more than a year continued to fight with the French against William. Then, at the beginning of 1696, his father decided to send him secretly to England to report on the situation there. Hardly had he landed, than William issued a proclamation offering the reward of £1,000 for his arrest.

Berwick's own account of what he did was: 'King James had privately concerted measures for an insurrection in England, whither he had sent a number of officers; his friends there had found means to raise two thousand horse there well appointed, and even regimented, ready to take the field on the first notice [under Sir John Fenwick]. Several persons of the highest distinction had also engaged in the business; but all were unanimously agreed not to throw off the mask before a body of troops was actually landed in the island. The Most Christian King readily consented to supply them; but he insisted that previous to the embarkation, the English should take up arms, not choosing to risk his own troops without being sure of finding a party there to receive them.'

Berwick had therefore the difficult task of convincing the loyalists in England to start the insurrection without James and his troops to lead them—a proceeding which they naturally refused. And, indeed, Berwick saw their point: 'I had several conversations with some of the principal noblemen; but it was in vain that I made the strongest representations I could think of, and urged the necessity of not letting slip so fine an opportunity. They continued firm in their resolution not to rise until the King of England had landed with an army. To say the truth, their reasons were good; for it is certain that, as soon as the Prince of Orange had discovered their revolt or had information of the design (which could not remain long concealed considering the preparations that would be necessary for transporting the troops), he would immediately have ordered out a fleet and blocked up the sea-ports of France; by which means the insurgents would have found themselves obliged to risk a battle with their raw, undisciplined troops against a good army of tried and experienced soldiers, and they must inevitably have been destroyed.'

The risk of recognition that Berwick ran in England (where, only eight years earlier, he had been a prominent figure at Court) was too great for him to prolong his stay for more than a few days. He was, in fact, on one occasion recognized in spite of his disguise, but the man put him immediately at his ease by whispering 'God speed you in all your enterprises,'—a sentiment which was probably representative of the country as a whole. On the other hand, Berwick's own ingenuousness in the matter of secrecy was partly to blame for his danger. Dressed in a French uniform suit and a blue cloak, he bought a pair of silk stockings in a hosier's in the New Exchange and paid for them from a purse full of louis d'ors. The shop-woman, naturally suspicious, informed the authorities.

Like the other followers of James, Berwick made use of the isolated house in Romney Marsh belonging to a farmer named Hunt, who made his real living by smuggling. Hunt was, as the event proved and as might have been predicted, anything but reliable; but Berwick was able to make his way from there, guarded by a loyal captain and his troop, to the lugger waiting off the Sussex coast to take him back to France.

Berwick escaped just before the betrayal of the so-called 'Assassination Plot' (which was, in fact, a kidnapping plot) led to the arrest of many of King James's partisans, including, eventually, Sir John Fenwick, who knew nothing about it.

[iii] The 'Assassination Plot'

It is unnecessary to assure anyone with the slightest knowledge of the character of King James II that the idea of assassinating William was to the last degree abhorrent to him. When some scoundrel suggested it, he had him immediately arrested; and when he found that he had been represented, however guardedly, as possibly approving of it, he instantly dismissed the man who had so misrepresented him.

Kidnapping, on the other hand, had a different complexion; and I see no reason to suppose that James would not have rather enjoyed turning the tables on William by successfully carrying out the manœuvre which William had tried to practise on him in 1688 and which had failed only because of James's violent attack of nose-bleeding.* 'Kidnapping the King' might, in fact, almost be described as a favourite Stuart pastime, which had been practised with success on both James I

* See *James by the Grace of God*, p. 179.

when he was King of Scotland and Charles I when he was a prisoner of Parliament.

On the other hand, nothing could better suit William than an apparent (but unsuccessful) attempt at assassination, which would restore his popularity and utterly discredit James; and it was this that one of his *agents provocateurs*, an unpleasant desperado named Porter, who posed as a Catholic and a Jacobite, eventually engineered.

There was a third type of man, the conscienceless hanger-on at James's court or the young enthusiast, who was quite prepared for murder in a profitable or a godly cause; and men of this kind, discrediting the King they served, were also implicated in the politics of the day—as, throughout history, they as well as the honest men and the *agents provocateurs* have appeared in similar revolutionary situations.

It was one such, by the name of Crosby, a secretary under Lord Middleton, who in the spring of 1695 had come over to England with the news that King James had issued a commission for levying war and seizing William—which meant, in effect, procuring his assassination. He seemed surprised that the English Jacobites had not received the commission and insisted that he had seen James sign it before he left France.

The mythical commission, of course, never arrived and the idea of murdering William so shocked the English Jacobite gentlemen, including Sir John Fenwick, that no steps were taken in the matter. Indeed Fenwick's attitude was such that he could claim that it was he who 'partly by dissuasions and partly by delays' was the main preventer of the design. He suggested to his friends that one of them should go direct to James to ascertain the truth. Before he went, he told some of the more important Jacobites in England of his intention and they encouraged him, saying 'it would be a great service to inform King James what an infamy Crosby had thrown upon him and that he ought to be severely punished to prevent any such thing for the future.' The delegate 'affirmed to King James before Crosby what he had said. King James reproved Crosby and told him that he would no more be employed in his service.'

The delegate may have been Fenwick himself; but in any case Sir John had made his attitude to an attempt on William's life so unequivocally clear that when, a year later, a new 'Assassination Plot' was hatched, those involved in it were careful to exclude him from their counsels.

This plot of 1696, which has still many unsolved features, took place at the same time as the discussions about the intended Stuart insurrection with which Berwick and Fenwick were concerned. On the part of the genuine conspirators, who considered it (I think, rightly) as a kidnapping plot which had the approval of James II, it was a piece of monumental ineptitude, which played directly into the hands of Porter, William's *agent provocateur*. By its coincidence with the insurrection (and this was probably intended by William) it made a legitimate *coup* by loyalist gentlemen appear to be a foreign invasion relying on murder; for the general public, even if William's intensive propaganda had allowed them to, were not likely to discriminate between the two plans, utterly different though they were.

Impressed by the way in which Crosby had misrepresented him in 1695, James in 1696 chose the sixty-year-old Sir George Barclay, a Scot who had fought under Dundee at Killiecrankie and a man of unimpeachable honour, to carry his commission to his followers in England, giving them the authority to 'take arms and make war on the Prince of Orange' at the appropriate moment. They were also empowered 'to do such acts of hostility against the Prince of Orange ... as may conduce most to our service.' This was taken to mean that William might, if possible, be kidnapped.

The men Barclay gathered round him, through his contact with two of James's agents in London, Charnock and Parkyns, included Ambrose Rookwood, John Bernardi, Sir John Freind—respectively Brigadier, Major and Colonel—and others of proved physical valour to the number of forty, whom he called his Janissaries. Unfortunately for everyone, Barclay, though cautious enough to refuse to employ one of William's spies, Fisher, eventually fell in with Porter who had recently added to his *bona fides* from the Jacobite point-of-view by spending some weeks in prison for riotously loyal conduct on the Prince of Wales's birthday.

Though Barclay at first distrusted Porter as one given too much to drinking, he eventually not only gave him his confidence but adopted the plan which Porter obligingly outlined. On February 15, William had arranged to go hunting in Richmond Park. He was in the habit of going by road from Kensington to Turnham Green and there crossing the river in a boat. From the place where he was accustomed to land on his return a lane led to Turnham Green 'something narrow, with hedges and ditches on each hand, so that a coach and six horses cannot easily turn, at least on a sudden.' The forty 'janissaries' were to be in readiness in the various ale-houses and taverns scattered about the Green so that, on a signal, they could assemble when William's coach arrived, at which point it should be a comparatively simple matter to overpower the guards and kidnap the Prince.

Thus far the plan had been worked out when Berwick arrived in England and was told of it. 'Sir George Barclay, lieutenant of my troop of Life Guards,' he wrote, 'meeting one day at a tavern a Mr Porter, the latter said that to facilitate the intended insurrection he had thought of a scheme which would make the matter almost sure. He explained to him all the movements of the Prince of Orange and said that with fifty men he would undertake to beat off the guards and seize upon his person. Barclay communicated this to me; and though I did not look upon the affair to be as certain as they concluded it was, I thought myself in honour bound not to dissuade him from it; but one of the conspirators, terrified at the danger or in hopes of a reward, betrayed it, so that the design was frustrated, just at the instant it was to be carried into execution.'

Which was, after all, what might have been expected.

William duly went in state to the House of Lords, sent for the Commons and from the Throne informed them that, but for the intervention of Heaven, he would at that moment have been a corpse and the kingdom invaded by a French army. Some of the traitors were in custody and warrants were out for others. The Houses instantly voted a joint address in which they thankfully acknowledged the Divine Goodness which had preserved him to his people. They suspended Habeas Corpus, exhorted him to arrest anyone he regarded as dangerous and thoughtfully provided that they themselves should not be dissolved by his death. Meanwhile the common people reacting as might be expected to the words 'foreign invasion' and 'assassination' forgot their grievances and indulged in the usual concomitants of Protestant indignation in the way of pillage and panic which recalled the good old days of Titus Oates.

Many of the leading Jacobites were arrested, though Barclay as well as Berwick got safely to France. They were put on trial as quickly as possible so that they might be tried under the existing law of High Treason which denied the prisoner the right of knowing the crime he was accused of until he heard the indictment in court. This state of affairs had already been abolished in principle by an Act which was to come into force on March 25, 1696. Consequently as many as possible of the conspirators were put on trial and condemned before that date; though even those who were covered by the new procedure gained little benefit from an action whose conclusion was foregone. Porter, together with two informers, gave the convenient, necessary evidence which convicted them all. Charnock, King, and Keyes were the first to die, to be followed by Sir John Freind and Sir William Parkyns who were tried and condemned on March 23 and March 24 respectively.

As the two knights, unlike most of the others (but like Sir John Fenwick) were devout Anglicans, they were attended on the scaffold by three Church of England clergymen, whom in common with many more, including Archbishop Sancroft and Bishop Ken, had refused to break their oath of allegiance to James by swearing one to William. Their action moved Bishop Burnet, William's creature, to intense wrath. He recorded: 'All three of them [the nonjuring clergy] at the place of execution joined to give them public absolution, with an imposition of hands in the view of all the people: a strain of impudence that was as new as it was wicked. . . . Two of them were taken up and censured for it in the King's Bench, the third made his escape.'

After March 25, Rookwood, Cranburne, Lowick, Cook and Knightley were tried and condemned, Porter still obliging.

But Sir John Fenwick so far remained at liberty.

[iv] Fenwick's Arrest

In William's original proclamation, offering rewards for the capture of the 'wicked and traitorous persons' who had 'entered into a horrid and detestable conspiracy to assassinate and murder His Majesty's Sacred Person,' the name of Fenwick was absent. Berwick and Barclay and Parkyns and Rookwood and twenty-six others were mentioned, but not Fenwick who, as we have seen, though consulting Berwick on the insurrection, was ignorant of the kidnapping.

Yet in the indictment subsequently framed against him, the main charge was of 'compassing and imagining the death and destruction of His Majesty,' by which the 'Assassination Plot' was meant. And even the secondary insurrection charge was so worded that it emphasized, irrelevantly, the murder attempt—'adhering to his [William's] enemies, by consulting and agreeing with several persons (whereof some have been already attainted and others not yet brought to trial for their said treason) at several meetings to send Robert Charnock (since attainted and executed for High

187

Treason for conspiring to assassinate His Majesty's
Sacred Person, whom God long preserve) to the late
King James in France.'

In the opening speech against Fenwick in the House
of Commons, Sergeant Gould deliberately linked and
confused the two. Having spoken of the insurrection, he
said: 'That fell to Sir John Fenwick's part. As to the
assassinating part, you have had several examples
already. This we have evidence to prove; and if we
prove this matter as we have opened it, then I think
there is no person whatsoever but will agree that this
is high treason in the highest degree.'

The actual evidence given against Fenwick asserted
his presence in 1695 at a meeting of various of James's
sympathizers in England at which they decided to send
Charnock to France to consult the King about details
of the insurrection and report to him that the 2,000
horse were in readiness whenever he should need them.
At this meeting were the inevitable Porter and an ex-
actor who had once been kept by the Duchess of Cleve-
land named Cardell Goodman, popularly known as
Scum Goodman. It was on the words of these two alone
that the charge against Fenwick rested; and even these
referred only to the 'insurrection' meeting. Not even
Porter had the effrontery to suggest that he had any
knowledge of the Turnham Green affair.

During the high treason trials of February, March and
April, 1696, Fenwick was safely in hiding. Though he
had not been named in any proclamation, he knew that
ultimately he would be sought for and he decided (or,
possibly, had been ordered by Berwick and Barclay
before they left) to go to France until the hue-and-cry
was over. But, before he went, he determined to make

188

a last gesture to help those of his imprisoned colleagues who were still alive, in particular the Earl of Ailesbury. The witness who was sending one after another loyalist to death was Porter, whom Fenwick imagined to be a terrified renegade Jacobite and whom therefore he supposed that a passage to France, a pardon from King James and a substantial bribe could silence.

That May, from his hiding place, he got in touch with two Irishmen he could trust implicitly, Clancy and Donelagh, and gave them their instructions. The result may be told in Porter's own words to the House of Commons: 'I had a meeting with one Clancy, first in Mitre Court and afterwards at the King's Head Tavern by the Playhouse. At those meetings he proposed to give me 300 guineas to bear my charges to France and send me a bill for 300 more; and likewise that I should be allowed £300 a year. He said he had been with Sir John Fenwick, who desired him to make this proposal to me. I met him about seven or eight times. The day before I was to go I met with my Lady Fenwick. She said, what Clancy had proposed should certainly be made good. I received 300 guineas of Clancy and he brought me a letter which, he said, was written by Sir John Fenwick to King James on my behalf. I had it and read it before it was sealed up and he delivered it to the gentleman that was to go with me, one Captain Donelagh. The contents, as much as I remember, was, He desired His Majesty, by reason that my going away was to save my Lord Aylesbury and my Lord Montgomery etc. to pardon what I have done.'

At this point, after the three hundred guineas had been counted on the tavern table and Porter had pocketed them, the *agent provocateur* gave a signal, at which several messengers from the office of the Secretary of State rushed into the room, and arrested Clancy, who was eventually tried, convicted and pilloried. Porter had once again served his Dutch master well.

At the next sessions of the City of London, on May 28, Fenwick was indicted of High Treason, with Porter and Goodman supplying the evidence. And, at this point, since no further service could be rendered by him in England, Fenwick made his final preparations for crossing to France. He left his hiding place and went to the usual rendezvous at Romney Marsh where, though Hunt's establishment had been broken up, he was confident of finding shelter till the boat arrived. But just before he turned off the high road, he had the misfortune to run into an official who was on his way to London with two smugglers he had caught and who at once recognized him.

'It is Sir John Fenwick,' said the guard to his prisoners. 'Stand by me, my good fellows, and I warrant you you will have your pardons and a bag of guineas besides.'

Fenwick dashed through them, pistol in hand and, because he was better mounted, threw off their pursuit. But the hue and cry was up. The bells of all the little Marsh churches rang out the alarm, every hut was searched and at last Fenwick was run to earth in the cottage where he was to await the ship to safety. Just as he was arrested, indeed, she approached the shore, showing English colours, waited a little while and then, disappointed of her passenger, stood out to sea.

Sir John managed so far to elude the vigilance of his captors as to be able to scrawl a note to his wife: 'What I feared is at last happened; had I gone alone I had done it; but the other was betrayed from London.* It is God's will, so we must submit. I know nothing can save my life but my Lord Carlisle's going over to him [William] backed by the rest of the family of the Howards to beg it and offering that I will be abroad all his time, where I cannot hurt him; and that I will never draw sword against him. I must leave it to you what else to say. . . . The great care must be the jury, if two or three could be got that would starve the rest. Money, I know, would do it; but, alas! that is not to be had, nor shall I get enough for counsel. I beg of you not to think of being shut up with me; I know it will kill you, and besides I have no such friends as you to take care of my business; though it would be the comfort of my life, the little time it lasts, to have you with me; and I have this only comfort now left, that my death will make you easy. My dearest life, grieve not for me, but resign me to God's will. You will hear, as soon as they bring me to Town, where they put me and then I would have a servant or somebody with me. I am interrupted, so can say no more now. . . . '

When Fenwick arrived in London to be arraigned before the Lords Justices, he learnt that the letter had been intercepted and taken to Whitehall.

[v] Turning the Tables

Everything seemed lost. But it was not in Fenwick's nature to accept defeat, and his next move—though he knew it must mean inevitably his death—was a desperate

---

* This suggests—though the dates are rather confusing—that Fenwick was crossing at the same time as Donelagh and Porter should have done.

throw to retrieve the general situation. He approached Devonshire, the Lord Steward, and informed him that he threw himself entirely on William's mercy and would disclose everything he knew about the Jacobite plots to unseat William. He would even give a list of plotters.

William, at the moment, was in Holland, but Devonshire thought Fenwick's offer sufficiently important to delay the trial until William's pleasure was known. William, in reply, authorized him to take Fenwick's confession in writing and send it to him as quickly as possible.

So Fenwick, using the knowledge that Berwick had given him, made a list of those who had been intriguing with James for William's downfall—Churchill, Shrewsbury, Godolphin, Russell and their peers; in fact, almost the entire Government. He also suggested that 'the Assassination Plot' was planned by the Government. The resultant alarm and despondency, were it not for its tragic outcome, provides one of the most hilarious moments in seventeenth-century history. For everyone conversant with the real state of affairs knew the accusation was true. Even William knew it, for as Monmouth said of him: 'He pretends not to believe these charges and yet he knows' (and here Monmouth confirmed his assertion with a tremendous oath) 'he knows that every word of the charges is true.' Yet he dared not officially believe or admit it. He wrote back furiously: 'I am astonished at the fellow's effrontery. You know me too well to think that such stories as his can make any impression on me. Observe this honest man's sincerity. He has nothing to say except against my friends. Not a word about the plans of his brother

Jacobites.' The impression, nonetheless, was considerable, though the political and personal repercussions
belong rather to the history of William III's reign than
to a consideration of Fenwick's case. It is enough to
say that Shrewsbury was not seen again at Court, that
Godolphin was dropped from the Ministry and that
Churchill was temporarily disgraced.

William returned from Holland to find that the news
of Fenwick's confession had got abroad in the country.
Knowing the damage likely to be done by a full and
open enquiry, he ordered that Fenwick was to be tried
by the ordinary courts and the matter not debated by
Parliament. The accused statesmen, however, especially
Russell, wished the matter to be brought up in the
Commons and their honour publicly vindicated in
solemn debate. And they suggested that, as a prelude,
William should himself see Fenwick. Accordingly at the
beginning of November, Fenwick was taken from prison,
where he had been for five months, and interviewed by
William in the presence of some ministers and the Crown
lawyers.

'Your papers, Sir John,' said William, 'are altogether
unsatisfactory. Instead of giving me an account of the
plots formed by you and your accomplices, plots of
which all the details must be exactly known to you,
you tell me stories without authority, without date,
without place, about noblemen and gentlemen with
whom you do not pretend to have had any intercourse.
In short your confession appears to be a contrivance
intended to screen those who are really engaged in
designs against me and to make me suspect and discard
those in whom I have good reason to place confidence.
If you look for any favour from me, give me, this

G   193

moment and on this spot, a full account of what you know from your own knowledge.'

Fenwick said that this request took him by surprise and asked for time.

'No, sir,' said William. 'For what purpose can you want time? You may indeed want time if you intend to draw up another paper like this. But what I require is a plain narrative of what you yourself have done and seen; and this you can give, if you will, without pen and ink.'

At this, Fenwick refused to say another word.

'Be it so,' said William. 'I will neither hear you nor hear from you any more.'

Fenwick was thereupon taken back to Newgate to await his trial for High Treason. But next day it was discovered that a trial was impossible. Of the two necessary witnesses against him, 'Scum' Goodman had disappeared. Lady Fenwick had discovered a tougher man than Clancy named O'Brien, who, accompanied by one of the picked Jacobites, had met Goodman at the Dog in Drury Lane and offered him the alternative of going to France and enjoying an annuity or having his throat cut then and there on the spot. Goodman chose France and O'Brien did not leave him till he was safely at St Germains.

[vi] The Bill of Attainder

The immediate reaction to Goodman's disappearance was the usual 'anti-Popish' outcry. A human head was found severed from its body and so mutilated that it was unrecognizable. Obviously Goodman had been foully

194

murdered by Papists. A little enquiry, however, in Goodman's usual haunts revealed the undoubted fact that he had chosen to go away and a Royal proclamation promptly appeared offering a reward of £1,000 to anyone who should stop him. But by this time Goodman was beyond William's reach.

Macaulay's pen, indignant for William, has recorded the ensuing dismay: 'This event exasperated the Whigs beyond measure. No jury could now find Fenwick guilty of high treason. Was he then to escape? Was a long series of offences against the State to go unpunished merely because to those offences had now been added the offence of bribing a witness to suppress his evidence and to desert his bail? Was there no extraordinary method by which justice might strike a criminal who, solely because he was worse than other criminals, was beyond the reach of the ordinary law? Such a method there was. . . . To that method the party that was now supreme in the State determined to have recourse.'

On November 5—an appropriate date—the Commons ordered Fenwick to be brought to the Bar of the House and, uncertain what other tricks the extraordinary man had up his sleeve, added a special caution that he should have no opportunity of making or receiving any communication, oral or written, on his way from Newgate to Westminster. When he arrived, strongly guarded, he was three times exhorted to confess his crimes. Three times he refused, giving his reasons cogently enough: 'I was in hopes that His Majesty would have informed the House himself. He hath all that I know. My circumstances are hard. I am in danger every day to be tried and I desire to be secured that what I say shall not rise up in judgment against me.

It is hard to make me accuse myself under these circumstances and very hard to put it on me now.' He remained painfully unimpressed by the Speaker's assurance: 'You have no reason at all to apprehend that you shall suffer anything if you make a full and free discovery here. No man that ever did so, and dealt candidly with this House, ever did.'

Fenwick's courteous but adamant refusals to implicate anyone at last exasperated the House and the Speaker rapped out: 'Sir, you know what the House doth expect. You must either give them satisfaction in it or withdraw.'

He withdrew and a motion was immediately carried to proceed against him by Bill of Attainder—that is to say, merely to declare that he was guilty without the necessity of proving it and to pass this decision by a majority, like an ordinary Government Bill.

For three weeks, the outnumbered Tories fought tenaciously to prevent the Bill's passage. However they may have disagreed with or even disliked Fenwick, they saw the action as a sacrifice of every principle of justice. Sir Godfrey Copley put it succinctly: 'I dread the consequence of this for our nation in general and for our posterity. It is not Sir John Fenwick's life I argue for. I do not think it worth a debate in this House* nor the consideration of so great an assembly; but I do say, if this method of proceeding be warranted by an English parliament, there is an end to the defence of any man living, be he never so innocent.' Young Foley, the

---

* When Lord Cutts subsequently reproached him for this remark, saying: 'I think the life of a gentleman may be thought worth ours,' Copley hastened to explain that he meant 'that, Sir John Fenwick considered in his single capacity, I did not think it was worth the while of this House to act in their legislative capacity on him.'

Speaker's son, contemptuously disposed of those who had argued precedents from the Earl of Strafford's case and the Duke of Monmouth's and others within living memory: 'There hath been no precedent that comes up to this—that we should pass a bill to attaint Sir John Fenwick because he will not give evidence or because there is no evidence against him. If Sir John Fenwick is to be hanged because there is but one witness against him, any man in the world may; and then I think every man's life depends on whether this House likes him or not.'

One of the most balanced speeches was made by Sir Francis Winnington, who twenty years before had been Attorney-General to King James II when he was Duke of York. It was nearly eleven at night when he rose to speak and the debate had been proceeding since eleven in the morning, so the old lawyer, who was now M.P. for Tewkesbury, made his points as tersely as possible. From the 230 columns which the report of the debate occupies in *State Trials*, it is worth quoting him, substantially in full.

'I shall trouble you but a little while, it being late,' he said, 'but, gentlemen, seeing it is an extraordinary case, I shall give my reasons why this Bill ought not to be committed; for every Member here is now a judge and he must take the blood of this gentleman upon him, either to condemn or acquit him, though I must confess I have been amazed to hear the doctrine preached that every man, as he is satisfied in his private conscience, ought to judge this man guilty!

'I desire to know by what authority we sit here? We sit here and have a legislative authority and it is by the King's command we come together. But at this time we are trying a man for his life; and therefore I humbly conceive that we ought to proceed according to what is alleged and proved—"secundum allegata et probata" —and if any man in his private opinion says he is guilty he is not acting by the commission by which he sits here. For to tell you of the "Lancashire Plot" or that a man shall not be dealt with this way hereafter seems to be an argument to inflame but having no bearing on the question.

'I agree with all the precedents, good and bad, that have been cited and do not question that in extraordinary cases it is in the legislative power of Parliament to look after the safety of the Kingdom; but I shall submit why this does not fall in that category.

'You have one witness, but I do not apprehend you have one good witness, for you must consider what Porter says upon his word; and I appeal to you, if you take what he says upon his word, did you ever know of a Bill of Attainder brought against any man on a bare affirmation? No! In that case, you should have turned it into an Impeachment, if the thing looked probable, and then you would have witnesses upon oath. . . . The ancient method of Bills of Attainder used to be first by the impeachment of the person and then to turn it into a Bill of Attainder.

'Next, look what is insisted on by the King's Counsel and recited in the Bill—that there was a bill of indictment found by the oath of two witnesses, Goodman and Porter. Under favour, I think they are not to be accounted witnesses in the point, because it is natural justice in all courts of the world that, if a man be accused as a malefactor, he has the liberty to cross-examine the person who accuses him. Now we all know very well

198

THE INNOCENCE OF SIR JOHN FENWICK

that Bills of Indictment, when they are found by the Grand Jury, never allow the prisoner to put cross-questions, because a Bill of Indictment is only an accusation. And, if an accusation alone is sufficient, who can be innocent? In this case, the oath of Porter that was given to the Grand Jury is not an oath on which you can put any value.

'Next, Sir, consider the paper of Goodman, which you would read, and consider the validity of that. Goodman being now absent, the prisoner has no opportunity for cross-examination. I beseech the House to consider the ill consequences of this. Any Minister of State may come and get an examination before a Justice of the Peace or Secretary of State, and the witness is conveyed away and a Bill of Attainder is clapped on the man's back and the statement shall be read as evidence against him. He is but half a witness —and a witness to an accusation, not a witness in a trial.

'Now I come to Sir John Fenwick's particular case. Sir John Fenwick is indicted, issue is joined and he has notice of his trial. One of the witnesses goes away. No man can tell why he went. (I may believe why, in my private opinion, but that is not my judicial knowledge.) Has it ever been known that when any man has been indicted and issue joined, a Bill of Attainder has been brought against him because his trial was deferred? Here are plots against the Government, and it may be forty are arrested for them. In the case of twenty, there may be two witnesses, but the others may have the good luck to have only a single witness against them. Will you have Bills of Attainder against all the rest?

'If this had been an extraordinary case, wherein the

Government had been particularly concerned, it might have weighed with you. But no man can show me any precedent for a Bill of Attainder except where men of great power were concerned to subvert the government. But what is Sir John Fenwick's case? He is in custody and the plot has been detected. If he had run away, you might still suppose he was plotting against the Government because he was fled from justice.

'Gentlemen say the Government *is* concerned. So it is in every felony and particular treason; but must there therefore be a Bill of Attainder to punish it? When there is a Bill of Attainder, it must be because of an immediate danger that threatens the government established that such a man is attainted. But I do not see that any of these circumstances apply to Sir John Fenwick.

'All men agree that this is an extraordinary way of proceeding. Then the question is: Is Sir John Fenwick's case extraordinary or is he anything more than a common malefactor who is in a wicked conspiracy? For myself, I cannot agree that this case of Sir John Fenwick's is so extraordinary that, unless he is hanged, the Government will fall.

'And, under favour, once a precedent is established, who knows what Time may produce from it? It may be that after the death of His Majesty who came to restore our liberties, we may have wicked Members and Members chosen as in Henry VI's time.* Sir John Fenwick's may be the condition of every subject in England.

* That is to say, by the victorious side in a Civil War. Winnington's parallel is here exact, since a restoration of James II could have resulted in similar acts of Attainder, on the precedent of Fenwick's, being legally used against all the Members of Parliament who were now voting for it!

'We must govern the power of Parliament by reason and common justice; and, as there is no urgent necessity to use this extraordinary remedy, I am against this Bill because it may be dangerous to posterity.'

When he sat down, Sir Thomas Littleton, one of the most active of the Whigs who was shortly to become Speaker of the House of Commons, sprang to his feet to make an objection. It was he who, urging the Commons not to 'consider little niceties' had tried to inflame them against Fenwick by talking of 'plot upon plot' and adding that he had heard so much gossip about the 'Lancashire Plot' that if anyone voted against the Bill, their constituents would be sufficiently incensed that their candidature would probably not be renewed at the next election. Littleton now said that Winnington had accused him of irrelevance in mentioning the 'Lancashire Plot' and that, if it came to a matter of irrelevance, 'I have heard him several times bring his wife and children into his speeches to no purpose at all.'

'I have a wife and children and that gentleman none,' Winnington replied. 'Therefore I think I may make use of that expression.'

The next speech was by Sir Thomas Seymour, who, having reminded the House: 'You may judge the prisoner, but others will judge you,' pointed out that, 'upon the whole there has been so much said by the counsel for the prisoner and so little said by the counsel against him that there is not evidence enough for you to proceed.'

The outspoken 'Jack' Howe (so known to distinguish him from his contemporary the Dissenting divine, John Howe) who had once been in William's household and, appalled by what he had seen and heard there, had severed his connection with both Court and Government, put the matter realistically: 'I believe, if Sir John Fenwick had been told when he was Major-General of King James's army that I should come here to sit upon his life, he would have laughed at it and thought it impossible. But the contrary has happened. And I have seen parties hang one another with such violence, I pray God we may keep from it. I do not know; we are all concerned in some measure. It has been the unhappiness of this nation that, at one time or another, everyone has been concerned in such a way as they could have a proceeding of this sort brought against them.'

But even the reminder of what they all knew—that this was an act of vengeance in a revolutionary situation—had no effect. Indeed, Howe's speech, by its very honesty, may have had the effect of hardening the Government in their determination to carry out William's orders.*

In his prison, Fenwick had no illusions. His wife had tried to comfort him by suggesting that the Commons would make another attempt to come to an understanding. But he knew that he would be pardoned only if he would betray his friends and wrote back: 'You speak as if you thought they would offer something to me. If they do, they shall never have another answer from me but what they have had.' After the Second Reading of the Bill in the Commons, he wrote: 'I am satisfied that nothing can save my life. There can be but one Reading more and then it goes up to the Lords. I

---

* Macaulay's sneer at Howe is most revealing: 'He was what is vulgarly called a disinterested man; that is to say, he valued money less than the pleasure of venting his spleen.'

believe now you have as little hopes as I have to succeed in that House better than I have done in the other. Tell me the truth, as you are my friend as well as my wife, and flatter me not. You give credit, I fear, to people who would see me dead and give you hopes till that hour come.'

On the day the Lords finally passed the Attainder, by a mere majority of six (which, if the Bishops had behaved legally and refrained from voting 'in a case of blood,' would have been only two.*) The Lords adjourned for a fortnight for the Christmas recess—an interval which was used by Fenwick's friends to plan his escape and by his enemies to put a strong military guard round Newgate.

In prison, Fenwick's one desire was to see his wife again. Throughout all his letters, this persists in a heart-breaking refrain: 'My dear life and soul, all my grief is I fear I shall never see you more, for if you hope for leave from the Lords I doubt you will be deceived, for though they should grant liberty for counsel and solicitor, yet they will say you must have leave from the King, the other being allowed in a judicial way, but yours as a favour; and what you may expect of that, you may judge. This is the only fear I have. Fear of death, I bless God I have none; but if I should not see you again, it would break my heart before I die. And I believe, too, they will be so cruel as not to allow me a desire [for you] to come to me, for this tyrant would destroy my soul as

* And as Churchill and Prince George of Denmark (Anne's husband who was entirely under his influence) as well as Sunderland and others who had been intriguing with James and had been listed by Fenwick also voted with the majority, the result was even closer than it seemed. Godolphin, to his lasting credit, voted against the Bill and Shrewsbury, of course, was absent.

well as my body. If I am once in his power, I expect no other.'

He wrote an apologia (which seems to be lost) to which he refers in another letter: 'I am writing a paper which I would leave with you which I would have you publish as much as you can safely when I am dead, but know not how to get it to you.'

The strain on Lady Fenwick, making her ill, was an additional anxiety. One letter, on the torn outside sheet of which is written in her hand: 'When the bill was passed,' shows his gallant attempt to cheer her: 'My dear life, I had yours dated last night and this by Dighton. He is in haste so I have only time to tell you I am glad to hear you are better. God be thanked for it. I am very well, too, as one in my condition can be. I long to know the particulars you mention. God in heaven bless my dear, dear life and send us a happy meeting.' But both knew that the consolation of meeting would be denied, and Fenwick dropped the pretence, setting himself to answer what may have been (we have not her letters) a threat of suicide after his death: 'My dear life, if you have that love for me you express, which I believe, in God I beg of you as I beg of Him that you will not grieve for me. Resign me to the will of God, offend Him not by your immoderate grief to destroy yourself. Indeed I am cheerful and all the sorrow I feel is the want of you: but how to have the comfort to see you I know not.'

On January 11, 1697, William gave his assent— which had never been in doubt—to the Bill. To Lady Fenwick's petition which she presented to him, throwing herself at his feet, he answered that he must consult his ministers. Her petition to the House of Lords that they would intercede with William to commute her husband's sentence to banishment took the Government by surprise and it was thrown out, after considerable difficulty in whipping up a majority, by only two votes. Alarmed by this, the Government saw that the Commons was properly prepared lest she should decide to appeal to them and when she did, on the last day of Fenwick's life, they refused her by a majority of forty-five.

Fenwick was executed on January 28, 1697, having been shriven by Thomas White, the nonjuring Bishop of Peterborough deprived of his See for refusing to acknowledge William's right to the throne. It was noted that Fenwick died with a composure and bravery which surprised even those who knew him.

[vii] Epilogue

It is, I hope, unnecessary to insist further on Fenwick's innocence on the one charge which is relevant to his condemnation—his participation in the 'Assassination Plot.' There is not a shred of evidence that he was even aware of it, though it is of course possible that Berwick may have mentioned it to him when they were discussing the general situation.

The story of this judicial murder has an epilogue which is one of the most edifying examples of unexpected justice in English history. Five years after Fenwick's execution, William was riding at Hampton Court, when his horse stumbled on a mole-hill. William broke his collar-bone and shortly afterwards died. Everyone knows of the famous Jacobite toast to the mole—'the little gentleman in black velvet.' But not everyone knows, I think, that the horse was Sir John Fenwick's favourite horse, Sorrel, which William had taken for his own after its master's execution.

6

THE MAN IN THE
IRON MASK

THE first known reference to the mysterious 'man in the mask,' who died in the Bastille on Monday, November 19, 1703 after thirty-four years in prison, is in a letter eight years later from the sister-in-law of Louis XIV of France to the mother of the future George I of England: 'A man has lived for long years in the Bastille, masked, and masked he died. Two musketeers were by his side to kill him if he unmasked. He ate and slept in his mask. There must, no doubt, have been some reason for this, as otherwise he was very well treated, well lodged and given all he wanted. He received Holy Communion in his mask; he was very devout and was perpetually reading. No one has ever been able to find out who he was.'

Another letter followed about a fortnight later with the information: 'I have just heard who the masked man who died in the Bastille was. His mask was not an act of barbarity. He was an English nobleman who had got mixed up in the Duke of Berwick's affair against King William and he was treated thus so that that King would never be able to find out what became of him.'

This, of course, was impossible, since the man had been in prison since 1669, the year before the Duke of

Berwick was born. But the letters are interesting, quite apart from their value as references, because they show by the eight-year interval how closely the secret had been kept even in Court circles and (by the reference to Berwick) how, from the first, the mysterious man was supposed to have some connection with England.

In the May of 1717, the youthful Voltaire made his first acquaintance with the Bastille and during his year's imprisonment there, he talked to people who had waited on the 'Mask' before his death thirteen and a half year's earlier. Though the prison officials no more knew the secret than did Louis XIV's sister-in-law, they were at least in a position to hear that kind of gossip which is valuable in any enquiry because it is probably founded on some kind of fact. And they knew the prisoner. Voltaire himself later elaborated and changed the story for his own purposes of propaganda against the Court and Dumas, seizing on it, immortalized it in that romance which generations of schoolboys and film-goers have assimilated to such an extent that, whatever the true solution, it is the Voltaire-Dumas theory which seems certain of popular survival.

According to this, the Mask was either the elder brother of Louis XIV or his twin, who was kept in prison with his features covered (the mask, incidentally, was not of iron but of black velvet—a simple and comfortable affair) lest there should be two apparent Kings of France, leading to disturbances in the State. Today, of course, this is dismissed as the romance that it is. Later discoveries have revealed Voltaire's many inaccuracies as well as his purpose in discrediting the monarchy by a story which played its small part in preparing a climate for the Revolution. But, at the time, it spread like wildfire and in 1801, nearly a century after the Mask's death, it was given its last and most fantastic twist.

The Mask, so the new legend ran, was really Louis XIV himself, kept in captivity, while on the throne was the illegitimate son of his mother, Anne of Austria and Cardinal Mazarin. And, while he was in prison at one of the earlier places of his incarceration on the Iles Sainte-Marguerite, in the bay of Cannes, he married. A son was born to him who was smuggled out of the castle-prison and taken to Corsica. The boy was given the name of 'de buona parte' (of good family) and became the grandfather of Napoleon. Thus, the Emperor Napoleon I was the rightful heir of the Bourbons!

The fantasy may have served Napoleon at the time— he was crowned Emperor three years after it was first put into circulation—and, when he was in such a position that he had all the State papers of France and of most of Europe at his disposal, he had a thorough search made in all the home and foreign correspondence of the period in the hope of discovering who the Mask really was. But in the end he had to own himself baffled and where he, given those resources, was defeated, it is improbable that anyone else can succeed.

Yet from the Louis XIV story one important lesson emerges. The first thing the historical detective (or, for that matter, any detective) has to learn is not to over-look the obvious and, in rightly dismissing the romances as being the wrong solution, one must be careful to notice that they contain the right clue. In all the thousands of learned pages written about the Mask and all the obscure candidates argued about and all the ingenuity expended in tracking down nonentities, this

obvious clue is monotonously forgotten—the simple fact
that the unknown man had to wear a mask, because,
if he did not, he would have been recognized. In other
words, he was exactly like somebody that everyone
knew. His face was as well known as, for example,
King Edward VII's face would have been in England
two hundred years later. If the Mask were not Louis
XIV or his brother, he must have been at least someone
who resembled him. And this axiom which novelists
remember while historians forget, makes it possible to
discard at the outset most of the clever academic
solutions. The wearing of the mask was a precaution,
not a punishment; and the man, on every matter
unconnected with his identity, was treated with all
possible consideration. Though he was deprived of his
liberty, there was no question of endangering his life.
He had no friends or (apparently) relatives to be
interested in his survival, yet no recourse was had to
the convenient and conventional solution of 'died in
prison' to remove him.

Two centuries' research has established with certainty
one of his names—Eustache Dauger, a valet. M. George
Mongrédien in his *Le Masque de Fer*, published in 1951,
which gives an admirable summary of all the candidates
and all the evidence, has confirmed incontrovertibly,
in my opinion, that the Mask (who must be the one
survivor of five prisoners originally in charge of M. de
Saint-Mars at Pignerol in 1681), was Dauger, and not
Matthioli. He thus confirms Andrew Lang's identification published in *The Valet's Tragedy* in 1903. And for
many years before that, it was recognized that the Mask
must have been either Dauger or Matthioli.

Count Matthioli was the secretary of the Duke of

Mantua, who, in 1679 was kidnapped by the French and imprisoned in the mountain fortress of Pignerol, near Turin, then on French soil, for having betrayed secret negotiations between the Duke of Mantua and Louis XIV. There was no secret about him. A book about him was published in 1682 and the matter was a subject of newspaper comment in 1687. As Lang says rightly, 'for years after his arrest, he was the least mysterious of State prisoners' and, in fact, the only reason for his identification with the Mask is that it is impossible to *prove* whether it was he or Dauger who died at the Iles Sainte-Marguerite in 1694. The argument that the Mask was buried under the name of 'Marchiel' is, considering that all State prisoners were buried under false names, hardly evidence, even if 'Marchiel' is a version of 'Matthioli.'

Without going into the complex details of the various arguments, one may say that today, thanks to M. Mongrédien, Dauger's claim is not likely again to be challenged—adding, for myself, that, had the simple point of the necessity of the *mask* been allowed for, the candidature of the well-known Matthioli could never have been seriously advanced.

The 'man in the iron mask' is, therefore, the valet, Eustache Dauger. But who is Eustache Dauger? No one. The name, indeed, is the really impenetrable disguise. One knows of him exactly nothing. 'You raise the mask,' as M. Mongrédien says, 'and behind it you find a prisoner without a record and without a face.' It is, indeed—but the French expresses it better than a translation: 'C'est par trop irritant et decevant!'

[ii] The valet, Eustache Dauger

ON July 19, 1669, Louvois wrote to Saint-Mars, in charge
of the prison at Pignerol that the King's lieutenant at
Dunkirk was bringing him an important prisoner—a
valet named Eustache Dauger. Though he might seem
of no great importance, as far as worldly position was
concerned, he was one whom it was vitally necessary
for the King's service to guard with all the precautions
that could possibly be devised. 'It is of the first importance that he is not allowed to tell what he knows to
any living person, either by writing or by any other
means. I am informing you of this in advance so that
you can prepare some lodging for him where no one can
pass his windows and where there are enough doors to
ensure that the sentinels outside the most remote can
hear nothing he says. You must yourself take to him,
once a day, the day's necessities and you must never
listen, under any pretext whatever, to what he may
want to reveal to you. You must threaten him with
death if he ever opens his mouth to you on any subject
but his day-to-day needs.'

Saint-Mars obeyed his instructions, prepared a safe
prison and, in the hearing of the Lieutenant de Vauroy,
Dauger's escort across France from Dunkirk, told him
that he would run him through with his sword if he
made any attempt to impart any secret to him. The
valet was safely in prison by August 24, and on August
31, Saint-Mars reported to Louvois that everyone at
Pignerol thought he must be a Marshal of France—an
estimate, it seems to me, which must have been based
on Dauger's age and bearing, as reported by the guards
who came silently in contact with him.

The search for the identity of Dauger leads backwards
—and to England. Charles II was immersed in the
negotiations with his cousin, Louis XIV, for the secret
Treaty of Dover by which the English King, with the
aid of French money, hoped to be able to establish
England once more as a Catholic monarchy instead of
a Protestant plutocracy and extricate himself from being
the virtual prisoner of Parliament. Louis, on his part,
wanted Charles's support, or at least, his neutrality in
his war with the Dutch. In what was one of the greatest
diplomatic duels of that century, the question resolved
itself into 'how much pressure Charles could put on
Louis by a tacit threat to make terms with Parliament,
and how far Louis could compel Charles to go in
that direction without the situation becoming too
dangerous.'

In the tortuous negotiations, one chief ambassador
was, it will be remembered, Charles's favourite sister
'Minette,' who was also Louis XIV's sister-in-law; but,
just as there were, on the surface, the ministers of both
countries, acting openly as regards part of the Treaty, so
there were, well below it, other mysterious go-betweens
to whom, even today, with so much documentation at
our disposal, we have no clue. And, among them, was
an elusive figure to whom Charles referred as 'the Italian'
(which may merely mean 'man from Italy') in a letter
to Minette written on the evening of January 20, 1669:
'I had written thus far when I received yours by the
Italian whose name and capacity you do not know,
and he delivered your letter to me in a passage where
it was so dark as I should not know his face again
if I saw him.' It is at least possible that this man,
who was apparently unknown even to Minette, is

the same mysterious, unidentified person of whom a year earlier—on December 27, 1667—Charles had mentioned: 'You know how much secrecy is necessary for the carrying out of the business and I assure you that nobody does or shall know anything of it but myself and *that one person more*, till it be fit to be public.'

One of the more bizarre figures of the time who was used as an envoy by Charles and Minette was l'Abbé Pregnani. He was among other things an astrologer to whom the Court naturally applied for racing-tips. In one of his letters, Charles tells his sister: 'I came from Newmarket the day before yesterday, where we had as fine weather as we could wish, which added much to the horse-races. L'Abbé Pregnani was there most of the time and I believe will give you some account of it, but not that he lost his money upon confidence that the stars could tell which horse would win, for he had the bad luck to foretell three times wrong and Monmouth had such faith in him that he lost his money.' Pregnani, a man of extremely dissolute habits, who found the stars also foretold that he would one day be Pope, died in Rome at the end of 1678. It seems unlikely that he was trusted with any profound secrets. But might he not have been a 'cover' for the mysterious man whom Minette did not know and whom Charles, in the darkness of the passage, did not see?

Because the theory that Pregnani and Dauger were one and the same was, in 1912, shattered (by the discovery that Pregnani was safe in Rome from 1674, till his death, when Dauger was certainly in prison), it has been unwarrantably assumed that there was no connection between the two. But this seems to me to be a complete *non sequitur*. Why should Dauger—assuming he is the mysterious stranger—not have been posing as Pregnani's valet? Such a hypothesis, not in itself unreasonable since it would be bordering on the eccentric if the Abbé had no servant, preserves intact the discovery which is the most brilliant single contribution to solving the mystery. For it has been discovered that Charles himself issued a passport to Pregnani on July 15, 1669; the Abbé left England on the 16th, arrived at Calais on the 17th and on the 19th Louvois wrote to Saint-Mars the letter I have quoted telling him of Dauger's arrest in the neighbourhood of Dunkirk and his dispatch to Pignerol. The coincidence is, to say the least, curious, nor does it seem to me that its relevance is really affected by the discovery that Pregnani and Dauger are not, as was at first believed, one and the same.

But even if it be admitted that the Mask, 'Eustache Dauger,' was involved in the very dangerous secret negotiations between Louis XIV and Charles II, it still does not explain why he had to wear a mask or give any clue as to who he really was; and the next stage of the enquiry must concern itself with his possible identity.

[ii] The Crisis of 1637

Some years ago, Lord Quickswood suggested to me a theory of the identity of the Mask which immediately made sense. Having heard it, I could not forget it and when, in 1955, I was preparing a broadcast on the Man in the Iron Mask, I wrote to him to ask if I might make it public. He was kind enough to give his permission, with this *caveat*—that there was no 'solid historic basis' to his 'ingenuities.' 'I regard them myself,' he said, 'as no more than a very good guess. I must admit that, when you come to hard evidence, there is nothing in favour of the theory that cannot very easily be overthrown: but I do think that it is a better case than any other case that has been put forward. No other theory answers any of the questions that may be put.'

In the broadcast, I mentioned Lord Quickswood's theory but did not adopt it as my own. Yet, subsequently, the more I tested it, the more likely it seemed. To say that it is a guess without any solid historic (in the sense of 'provable') basis is merely to say that it is like every other theory of the Mask's identity which has been or ever will be advanced. And, as on the one hand, it makes more sense than any alternative solution and, on the other—as I hope to show—there is no known evidence with which it is incompatible, I have now come to accept that inspired guess of Lord Quickswood as the solution I am myself prepared to defend. In a sentence, it is that the Mask was Louis XIV's father.

The events leading up to what the *Cambridge Modern History* describes as 'the unexpected, almost miraculous birth' of Louis XIV in 1638 were these. In 1637, the King and Queen of France, Louis XIII and Anne of Austria, had been married for twenty-two years and had lived apart for the last fourteen of them. There were no children. Without being on scandalously bad terms, they were known to have no great regard for each other and there were rumours that the King was impotent.* The real ruler of France at the time was, it will be remembered, the great Cardinal Richelieu.

The King, the Queen and the Cardinal seldom agreed on any topic; but it so happened that, in 1637, they all intensely wanted the same thing—an heir to the throne of France. In the absence of a Dauphin, the next King would be Louis XIII's younger brother, that lamentable young man, Gaston, Duke of Orleans. For different reasons, King, Queen and Cardinal all loathed him and were all to the last degree apprehensive of his succession to the Throne. Louis XIII was, though not old, weak and ill and not expected to live long. All his principles of government were certain to be abolished and all his work undone should Gaston succeed him. Gaston would probably execute Richelieu and certainly remove Anne from any influence.

In the circumstances, the Cardinal exerted himself to reconcile the King and Queen, who met at one of his country houses. It was shortly announced that the reconciliation had succeeded and that the Queen was

* It may be of some interest that the last attempt at a solution of the Mask in France, in 1934, M. Pierre Vernardeau's *Le Médicin de la Peyne* rests on the assumption that Anne of Austria's doctor, when performing the autopsy on Louis XIII, discovered an 'ectopie des testicules,' which established scientifically the impotence of the King and, consequently, the illegitimacy of Louis XIV; and that the Mask was a man who knew the secret. The theory seems, according to M. Mongrédien, to have been demolished by M. Geoffroy Tenant de la Tour's nineteen-page pamphlet in reply, issued the same year, which, I fear, I have not read but which, from M. Mongrédien's description of it, appears conclusive in establishing that the particular doctor, Pardoux Gondinet, whom M. Vernardeau mentions, did not enter Anne's service until the year after Louis XIII's death and consequently could not have performed the autopsy. I am not certain, without seeing more of the evidence, that this really disposes of the cardinal point at issue—that the King was impotent —and it in no way affects Lord Quickswood's theory, which does not postulate impotence. He himself, in fact, does not believe it, but holds that Anne's second son, 'Monsieur,' was Louis's child.

pregnant. Gaston and his party were extremely sceptical and announced in advance that, if she was, the Cardinal must be the father. This, for many reasons, was extremely unlikely, though Richelieu thought the succession sufficiently important to make it prudent for him to show no special interest in the birth of the child and to be away in the country, far from Court, when it was born.

Anne's confinement was painful and difficult and it was noticed by those in attendance that Louis (who sat in a room next door to her bedroom) showed the utmost anxiety for the life of the child, but was quite uninterested in what happened to the mother. The child was a most magnificent specimen, very strong and as unlike Louis XIII as it was possible to be. He who as Louis XIV 'was to make a mark on history of almost unequalled physical and mental vigour,' was indubitably a very odd son for Louis XIII to have had—as Gaston and his supporters quite brutally noticed at the time.

'I am afraid that I cannot claim any direct historical evidence which would point further than these undoubted circumstances suggest,' Lord Quickswood wrote to me, 'but I cannot help asking what so able a man as Richelieu would have done when it was necessary for the King to have a son. Richelieu was unscrupulous, though not to the point of depravity; but he would certainly have felt justified in substituting someone as a father for the Queen's son, if this was the only way out of his difficulties. It is likely that in Paris at that time there were illegitimate descendants of Henry IV* and an able and unscrupulous man like

---

* 'Likely' seems to me a considerable understatement. Henri Quatre's illegitimate sons would, of course, be Louis XIII's half-brothers, though the obliging youth would probably be a grandson.

Richelieu, with boundless power at his command, might easily find a young man of seventeen or eighteen who was willing to play the splendid, if ignominious, part which was required. He would pick his man; he would persuade the Queen that union with this man was the only way out of their difficulties; and if the young man was good-looking and attractive, it was even possible that she would welcome him as a mate on those grounds. The circumstances that the reconciliation of the King and Queen took place at a country house of the Cardinal's would make it quite possible for the young man to be smuggled into the house and out again without the knowledge of anyone except the three great conspirators concerned. When success came and it was clear that the Queen was going to have a child, the young man would be loaded with money and persuaded to leave France for Canada. He would there reside until all three of the conspirators were dead. The Queen was the last to die, and probably from motives of chivalry the young man would say nothing as long as she lived, but when she was dead it would be natural for him to want more money than he had received and he would come to Europe fishing for gold. The ministers in charge of France at the time would quickly see the danger of such a claim as he might make, the more so because he had a marked facial resemblance to the King, Louis XIV.'

Lord Quickswood also cites the later investigation into the Mask's identity by Louis XV who announced that the man was imprisoned because he had a remarkable resemblance to the Royal Family and had used it in a mischievous and seditious manner; and the well-known episode (which, in spite of the fact that Voltaire

uses it, seems to be true) that during his imprisonment
in the Iles Sainte-Marguerite fortress, the Mask once
wrote something with a steel fork on a silver plate and
threw it out of the window so that it fell on the beach.
A fisherman picked it up and brought it to the castle,
whereupon Saint-Mars asked if the fisherman could
read. When the fisherman answered 'No,' Saint-Mars
said: 'It is lucky for you that you cannot, for it would
have been necessary to put you to death if you could.'

I have the greater confidence in Lord Quickswood's
theory because it is he, as himself a statesman and, even
more, as a member of the great 'ruling house' of Cecil,
who enunciates it. One may have various views on the
character of the Elizabethan founders of the Cecilian
dynasty (for that term is not too strong), but there can
be no difference of opinion on the fact that it has for
nearly four centuries, been one of the finest families of
statesmen in Europe, continuously concerned in the
art of government. And any statesman, particularly a
Cecil, is not likely to view history with the same eyes as
a professional recluse counter-checking manuscripts or
an earnest history teacher trying to instruct his charges
in the principles of good citizenship. Neither of these
would probably assume that it was a natural thing for
Richelieu to act in the way that Lord Quickswood
(and, it may be added, the ordinary common sense of
any man of the world) assumes that he acted. But that
only adds another count to one's indictment of the
academics who fail to understand that 'history' and
'life' are synonymous terms. In the nature of things
there can be no 'documentary evidence' that Louis
XIV's 'almost miraculous birth' was compassed in that
way; but that a Cecil assumes that that is how Richelieu

would have arranged it, is, for me, as good as any such evidence and better than most.

The one weakness of this solution, which its author admits, is that the Mask, if he were Louis XIV's father, would have lived till the age of eighty-three. 'It is not impossible that he may have done so,' writes Lord Quickswood, 'but it is certainly an element of improbability that must be weighed against the theory, with which otherwise everything corresponds.' Thus the next part of the enquiry must concern the Mask's age.

[iii] How old was the prisoner?

The one documentary reference to this is in the parish register of the church where he was buried on November 20, 1703 under the name of 'M. de Marchiel' Here it is given as 'about forty-five.' Even if one did not know, from other cases, that State prisoners were given false names and ages, this is patently nonsensical, as it would make him about eleven at the time of his arrest at Dunkirk. There is, therefore, no direct evidence of his age; but if he were the father of Louis XIV he would have been about forty-nine at the time of his arrest—which would not be incompatible with the rumour at Pignerol that he was a Marshal of France.

The Mask was in four prisons—at Pignerol from 1669 till 1681; at Exiles from 1681 to 1687; at Sainte-Marguerite from 1687 till 1698 and in the Bastille from 1698 till his death in 1703. At Exiles, if he were Louis's father, he would have been in his sixties. The nephew of the Lieutenant of that prison later wrote: 'My uncle, told me how, in order to see the Mask, he had once taken the place of a sentinel and watched outside his prison. He saw him at night through the window, a tall well-made man and still vigorous in spite of his grey hair.'

This incident probably occurred at the beginning of 1687. Saint-Mars had been promoted from Exiles to Sainte-Marguerite and had asked permission to go and see his new domain. He explained that he had to leave the Mask behind but 'has forbidden the Lieutenant even to speak to that prisoner.' At Sainte-Marguerite, Saint-Mars had a new prison built specially for the Mask with large, sunny rooms at the cost of 5,000 livres (which may, surely, be interpreted as a concession both to his rank and his increasing age). When, finally, Saint-Mars went to take up his command there in the May of 1687, the Mask accompanied him in a sedan-chair. The obvious means of transit was a litter, but a litter might have broken down and the prisoner have then been seen. As it was, after twelve days travel in a closed chair, the Mask was nearly dead (which, though such an experience might have been too much for many people, suggests an old rather than a young man).

There is another, and to my mind, more conclusive argument about the Mask's age. In the controversy, to which I have referred, between those who claim Dauger as the Mask and those who support the claims of Matthioli, there is one passage which turns on the interpretation of the word 'ancien.' From the time of Dauger's arrest till his death, as we have seen Saint-Mars was uninterruptedly in charge of him. As the Governor was sent from Pignerol to Exiles and from Exiles to Sainte-Marguerite and from Sainte-Marguerite to the Bastille, so Dauger went with him. But Matthioli

THE MAN IN THE IRON MASK

did not go to Exiles, but remained at Pignerol until 1694, when he was moved to Sainte-Marguerite and thus, after a seven-year separation, came once more under Saint-Mars's surveillance.

On November 17, a Government official wrote to Saint-Mars: 'All you have to do is to watch over the security of all your prisoners, without ever explaining to anyone what it is that your old prisoner has done (sans vous expliquer à qui que ce soit de ce qu'a fait votre ancien prisonnier).' Saint-Mars on his part regularly mentioned in his letters 'mon ancien prisonnier.' The Matthiolists argue that this means 'my erstwhile prisoner: he who was left at Pignerol and is now restored to me.' The Daugerites insist that it must mean 'my prisoner of long-standing.' As between them, in this particular argument, there is no doubt that the latter are right—especially as, apart from anything else, Matthioli was not imprisoned at all till ten years after Dauger. The 'ancien prisonnier' must be Dauger. But why need 'ancien' mean 'of long-standing' or 'senior?' Why cannot it merely mean 'old?' And in the context, were it not for the strange and untenable theory that Matthioli might have been the Mask, why should anyone have supposed it meant anything else?

The first time the adjective appears in the correspondence between Saint-Mars and government officials is in 1693—that is to say, when the father of Louis XIV would have been about seventy-three—and it continues till the end. It even appears in the journal of du Junca, the Lieutenant of the Bastille, (to whom 'ancien' could not possibly have either meaning applied in the Dauger-Matthioli controversy,) when he notes where 'l'ancien prisonnier' is lodged. Must it not mean merely that the Mask was an old man—a probability reinforced by the fact that he spent his time quietly reading or at his devotions and that, one morning after Mass, he felt a little unwell and died quietly the same evening, after making his confession, without having had any disease? So a man of eighty-three might die.

Thus it seems to me that the age of Louis XIV's father, far from impugning Lord Quickswood's theory, actually supports it; and that if one merely looks at the known evidence (without wresting 'ancien', for controversial reasons, to mean something that it obviously does not mean), an old man is, in fact, postulated after 1693. Indeed, as far as I can see, the only reason that the Mask was ever thought of as being young is that he was described as a 'valet' which, by a conventional association of ideas, suggests youth. Had he been described as a 'butler,' it would, with equal illogicality, have been assumed that he was old.

It is, therefore, possible to say of Lord Quickswood's 'inspired guess' that it explains every aspect of the mystery—the masking, the precautions against the telling of the secret, the considerate and respectful treatment of the prisoner. It tallies with the suggestion which, however romantically embroidered, has from the first been integral to the story—that there was some connection between the prisoner and the King. It provides as the reason why the prisoner was not simply killed, or at least allowed to die in prison, (which, considering the obvious danger of his secret, is a minor mystery in itself) that Louis XIV could not, whatever the danger, commit parricide. Only one question remains to be answered to complete the solution; and that does not really concern Lord Quickswood's theory, which is already satisfied, but my own view, which postulates the visit to England as part of the story. Louis XIV's father could certainly have been 'Eustache Dauger, a valet'; but could he have been the mysterious messenger to Charles II?

[iv] Was 'The Mask' in England

There is no need to insist that any reconstruction of the Mask's life between 1637 and 1669 must be purely imaginary. Lord Quickswood's suggestion that he would be banished to the French possession of Canada is likely enough, but, even if he delayed his return till the death of Anne of Austria, it is improbable that he would risk living in France, once he had made—if he did make—his attempt at blackmail. He would be much safer in, for example, Italy.

The more one considers his position, the more impossible, from a practical point of view, becomes the theory that he dared to visit France at all. His only asset was himself. His story alone, divorced from any proof, could be dismissed as a *canard*, which nobody would take seriously. And what proof could he supply except his own person—which would have resulted in instant arrest?

But there was one market in which he could sell his information at a high price. To Charles II of England, in his diplomatic duel with Louis XIV, the secret would have been invaluable. The 'Mask,' were he a grandson of Henri IV, would have been cousin to Charles, who was also a grandson of Henri IV; and he could, without too much difficulty, have established the authenticity of his story. The underworld ramifications of the secret treaty of Dover affected, at that moment, most of Europe. In Italy they had already produced the curious affair of James de la Cloche and there is nothing inherently improbable in the suggestion that 'Dauger' (whatever name he may have been going under) might have met Pregnani in Rome and thus gained entry into the secret labyrinth.

Such a theory also fits the odd fact that Minette did not know who he was when he went, in the ordinary course of the secret negotiations, to her brother. Minette, as the wife of Louis XIV's younger brother Philip who resembled Louis XIII as much as Louis XIV differed from him,* was the last person to be entrusted with that secret.

There is no need to pursue further what are only possibilities. The one point I wish to make is that the Mask's relation to the English diplomatic situation can be explained as well on Lord Quickswood's theory as on any other and better than on most, the conventional 'James de la Cloche' hypothesis included.

In conclusion, to quote from Lord Quickswood's letter: 'All the circumstances recorded in history about the Man in the Iron Mask do exactly correspond to what would have happened if he had been secretly father of the King. No doubt the thesis rests only on theoretical grounds, but those who reject it may be asked what other explanation can be given which is as plausible as this one. Why was he kept in prison instead

---

* It is this fact which makes Lord Quickswood reject the theory of Louis XIII's impotence, though to my mind it is not conclusive against it. There is no suggestion that the fathers of Anne of Austria's children were not Bourbons.

of being executed for treason? Why, above all, was he not allowed to show his face? Why was the secret of his birth such as could be written on a silver plate and yet be of such a character as would make it unsafe for the Government to leave alive the fisherman who had picked up the plate, if he had read it? That Louis XV found out nothing extraordinary is quite intelligible. Very few people would know the truth—perhaps none surviving at the time of his enquiry; and in any case, the truth (if it be what I suppose) would be the last thing that would be told to the reigning monarch of France. Nowhere, we may be sure, would it have been recorded: nowhere would it have been allowed to displace the plausible account that the prisoner was a mere adventurer, trading on an accidental resemblance to the royal family. But I must not overstate my case. The theory that the Man in the Iron Mask was really the father of Louis XIV is just an historical guess, of which it would be foolish to contend that there was any evidence greater than to justify its claim to be a better guess than any other.'

I hope I may claim to have shown in addition that what Lord Quickswood sees as the one weakness of the theory—the man's age—is really its strength; for the existing documents of the case support the contention that the Mask, who was quite certainly 'Eustache Dauger,' was almost certainly an old man. Nor does the theory involve the abandonment of the discovery that Pregnani, with a secret passport from Charles, arrived at Calais the day before 'Dauger' was arrested, about fifteen miles to the east of Calais, and almost in sight of the technical safety of the French border, to be sent, in the strictest custody to Pignerol, over 500 miles to the south. Indeed, if 'Dauger' was posing as Pregnani's 'valet,' it increases the value of that discovery by explaining why, as Pregnani was officially on the way to Paris, the 'valet' went in the opposite direction on landing in France.

The case rests.

THE DIAMOND NECKLACE

[i] Jeanne de la Motte

THE *Public Advertiser* of Friday, August 26, 1791, recorded: 'The noted Countess de la Motte, of Necklace memory, and who lately jumped out of a two-pair-of-stairs window to avoid the bailiffs, died on Tuesday night last, at eleven o'clock, at her lodgings near Astley's Riding School.'

Jeanne de la Motte, a descendant of the Valois, was thirty-four at the time of her death. As one of the chief actors in the Diamond Necklace affair—if not, indeed, the chief—she had been sentenced, five years earlier, to whipping, branding and imprisonment. Young Mr Eden, who was in Paris at the time as a special envoy had described the event in a letter to the twenty-seven-year-old Prime Minister, William Pitt: 'Madame de la Motte was called up at five and informed that the Court wished to see her. She had no suspicion of the judgment, which is not communicated here to the accused, except in the case of a capital sentence. She went in an undress, without stays, which proved convenient. Upon the registrar reading the sentence, her surprise, rage and shrieks were beyond description. The *bourreau* and his assistants instantly seized her and carried her into an outer court, where she was fastened to a cart with a halter round her neck. The *bourreau* talked to her like a tooth-drawer and assured her most politely that it would soon be over. The whipping was slight and *pro forma*, but the branding was done with some severity. It is a good idea that the V (*voleuse*) on her shoulders stands also for Valois.'

She was then imprisoned in the Salpêtrière.

At the time of her arrest, her husband and accomplice, the self-styled 'Count' de la Motte, had managed to escape to England, where on an earlier visit he had exchanged £10,371 6s. worth of the diamonds from the stolen Necklace for less dangerous jewels at Robert Gray's, the jeweller in New Bond Street. An attempt by French agents to kidnap him one evening as he came out of the Haymarket Theatre, convinced him that London was less safe than he had hoped and, after visiting Lancaster, Dublin and Glasgow, he settled in Edinburgh at the house of an old Italian teacher of languages. The French Ambassador in England, through his agents, offered the old man 10,000 guineas to arrange for him to be drugged and put aboard a French collier at South Shields. The ambassador paid in advance 1,000 guineas (less £63 which was his secretary's 'cut') but the Italian instead of fulfilling his bargain promptly shared the money with his intended victim and at the time of his wife's trial and branding in Paris, de la Motte was living, in comparative safety, at the corner of Charlotte Street and Rathbone Street in Soho.

During that autumn of 1786, he talked so openly about printing in England an apologia which would shake the French court that the Duke of Dorset, who was concerned with French affairs, wrote to Eden that a memoir was to be published about the Necklace affair which, as it was certain to contain nothing but falsehoods and calumny, the French Government should arrange to be answered immediately on its appearance by some clever journalist such as the editor of the *Courrier de l'Europe* (who was in French government pay).

Meanwhile, de la Motte started to implement his threat by writing to the *Morning Chronicle* a long letter in which he declared that, unless he received justice from the French authorities, he would consider himself free to publish letters which he fortunately had in his possession which would reveal the truth of the Necklace affair. 'For the purchasing of the Necklace I shall account in the clearest manner by *making mention of its real owner* who made my wife a present of some of the most brilliant diamonds which I sold in London as my property. By a concatenation of circumstances which happened pending the process, my wife and I were abandoned and inhumanly sacrificed. . . . I am not to be told that my memorial, if published, will, by the secret and curious anecdotes it contains, raise against me a host of powerful foes, who will not fail to seek for, and meet with, sufficient opportunity to wreak their vengeance on me. But what of that? My intentions shall have been fulfilled; and, whatever be my fate, I shall have the comfort of having left behind me an authentic justification, and of having unveiled the whole of the intrigue. And who knows I may be fortunate enough to hear one day or other, for the good of my country, that my memorial has opened the eyes of him who has been kept so long in the dark! [King Louis XVI.]

But for that I shall be told the memorial must not reach him and all avenues will be strongly beset. I am aware of it. But, on the other hand, I shall observe that there exists a powerful party, whose interests it is to forward it, who have been long employed in working a mine which only waits a favourable opportunity for explosion. To hasten this, if my memorial has, as it were, the effects of a match, I shall look upon all the misfortunes I have encountered as the path leading directly to that event.'

The 'explosion' was, of course, the French Revolution which started with the fall of the Bastille two and a half years later and there is no doubt that the eventual de la Motte memorial was indeed one of the 'matches' which touched it off. Though this could hardly have been foreseen by the French Court, the appearance of the 'Count's' letter (which was again published in the same paper two days later, this time in the original French, and sent in quantities to Paris) taken in conjunction with the Duke of Dorset's warning, which Eden had passed on to the highest quarters, created considerable consternation at Versailles, in particular among the friends of Marie Antoinette.

About four months later in the spring of 1787 (the exact date is in dispute) two of these friends, the Duchesse de Polignac and her sister-in-law, went to England, ostensibly to drink the waters at Bath, actually to come to terms with de la Motte through the agency of Georgina, Duchess of Devonshire. One suspects, from Marie Antoinette's letter to the Duchesse de Polignac enquiring whether she has received any benefit from the Bath waters that 'benefitting by the waters of Bath' was merely a code phrase for 'securing the memorial from de la Motte'; and, in the June of 1787, there appears in a letter to the King of Poland a report of the gossip at Versailles that the Duchess de Polignac has paid Count de la Motte four thousand louis for certain letters said to have been written by the Queen.

At the end of July, Jeanne de la Motte, having escaped from the Salpêtrière and for seven weeks eluded capture in France, arrived in London to add fuel to the already considerable flame.

In so far as the case of the Diamond Necklace is still a mystery, the question is: Who helped Jeanne de la Motte to escape and why? This remains the one enigma, for the idea that Marie Antoinette was in any way concerned in it has long been dismissed by all students of the matter. As Andrew Lang put it half a century ago: 'the pyramidal documents of the process, still in existence, demonstrate the guilt of the de la Mottes and their accomplices at every step and prove the stainless character of the Queen.'

Yet, in the last few hours of her life, Marie Antoinette, facing the revolutionary tribunal, had to answer the calumny, when the President asked her: 'Was it not at the Petit Trianon that you first met the woman de la Motte?'

'I never once saw her,' answered the Queen.

'Was she not your victim in the business of the famous Necklace?'

'She could not have been, as she was quite unknown to me.'

'So you persist in denying that you were acquainted with her?'

'Mine is not a system of denial,' said the Queen. 'What I have said is the truth. That, I will persist in.'

The great Mirabeau himself pronounced: 'The case of the Necklace was the prelude of the Revolution' and Saint-Just hailed it with: 'What a triumph for Liberal ideas! A Cardinal a thief! A Queen implicated! Mud on the crosier and the sceptre!'

And to this result, Jeanne de la Motte's memoirs, which she published once she was safe in England, contributed almost as much as the case itself. They gave the interpretation, the twist, which made it invaluable propaganda to the organizers of the Revolution. How could the French Government, which had been warned by English diplomatists, which had made such elaborate cloak-and-dagger plans to kidnap de la Motte, and the French Court, which had sent emissaries to 'benefit by the waters of Bath,' have permitted the escape of the most dangerous criminal in the case, once they had her safely in prison? Who engineered her escape?

But before examining the possibilities, it may be as well to refresh the reader's memory by giving a short resume of the famous 'Case of the Necklace.'

[ii] The Necklace

In the year 1772, King Louis XV was hopelessly at the mercy of his mistress, Dubarry. He regretted that he could not present her with a palace composed entirely of gold and precious stones. She announced her willingness to be satisfied instead with a necklace made of the finest diamonds which could be found. The Court jeweller, Böhmer and his partner, therefore scoured Europe for the stones and eventually 629 diamonds, of the finest water, were collected, mounted and strung together in this fabulous necklace. Unfortunately for Böhmer, at this moment the old King died of smallpox and the jewellers were left with it on their hands, with no prospect of a purchaser willing or able to pay the two million livres (which would be equal to about £2,000,000 in today's currency) that Louis had promised. And as Böhmer had got most of the diamonds on credit, to be paid.for when he was paid by the King, he faced virtual ruin unless the new King and Queen, Louis XIV and the twenty-year-old Marie Antoinette would buy it.

The Queen, though impressed by the diamonds, refused it—the thing was in ghastly taste and she had no desire for a necklace 'like a comforter'—and, when her husband offered to buy it for her, she forbade him on the grounds that France had more need of a ship of war than a set of jewels.

Böhmer was beside himself. He had sent his partner to all the other courts of Europe and he had brought the price down but there was still no prospect of a sale. For the next five years, whenever a Royal baby was born, the jeweller went to the palace in the hope that the Queen would change her mind and buy it for the christening festivities. In fact, it became a joke in Court circles and whenever anyone met Böhmer on the way to Versailles, they asked: 'Another Royal baby?'

At last, in 1777, Böhmer, who was almost ruined by the interest he had to pay (he had borrowed 800,000 livres from the Treasurer of the Navy), craved an audience, threw himself at the Queen's feet, sobbed considerably and threatened, if she did not buy it, to throw himself in the Seine.

'Get up, Böhmer,' said the Queen. 'I do not like such

scenes and honest people do not find it necessary to kneel. You know I have more than once refused the Necklace. Never mention the matter to me again. Try to break it up and sell it—but don't drown yourself over it.'

If Böhmer would have done practically anything to get the Queen to buy the Necklace, the Cardinal de Rohan, Grand Almoner of France, would have done anything merely to prevent her cutting him. Marie Antoinette loathed the tall stout handsome man of fifty or so who had been ambassador to her mother, the Empress's Court of Austria. She disliked him on every count, including his notorious lechery, and his selling of ecclesiastical preferments. Two anecdotes give a clue to the man better than any description. On one occasion in Vienna, he and his entourage, dressed in hunting costume, had broken through a procession of the Blessed Sacrament. On another, in France, he went riding in his carriage with his mistress by his side disguised as a young Abbé.

His Eminence Louis-René-Edouard de Rohan, Cardinal of the Holy Roman Church, Bishop and Prince of Strasbourg, Prince of Hildesheim, Landgrave of Alsace, Grand Almoner of France, Commander of the Order of the Holy Ghost, Commentator of St Waast d'Arras, Superior General of the Royal Hospital of the Quinze-Vingts, Abbé of the Chaise Dieu, Master of the Sorbonne, Member of the French Academy, etc., etc., etc. had only one ambition left—to get into the good graces of Marie Antoinette at least to the extent that, on the state occasions when she was bound to meet him in his official capacity, she would refrain from cutting him dead.

The third actor in the tragi-comedy was the Jeanne de Saint-Remy, with whom, under her married name of Countess de la Motte, the reader is already acquainted. She was descended from the Saint-Remy who was one of the illegitimate sons of Henri II and she never forgot her Valois blood. She was born at the château of Fontette near Bar-sur-Aube in 1756 to impoverished parents who sent her out to beg crying: 'Pity a poor orphan of the blood of the Valois: alms, in God's name!' The Marquise de Boulainvilliers, investigating her story, found that the claim was true, adopted her and sent her to be educated at a convent. Later she married one of her lovers—La Motte 'calling himself Count and to all appearance a stupid young officer of the *gendarmie*.' The pair lived in the way that might have been expected of them and, in 1781, again 'made prey' of the Marquise who was then at Strasbourg as a guest of Cardinal de Rohan and his friend and, in a sense, master, the strange and sinister Cagliostro, of whom more will be said later.

Jeanne de la Motte had the gift of charming people into believing almost anything she wanted them to believe. Without allowing for this, which is testified on all sides by contemporaries, her incredible story cannot be understood. She is, indeed, *the* 'confidence-woman' of history. And in due course, she made the Cardinal de Rohan believe that she had such influence with the Queen (whom she did not know) that she was able to restore him to the Royal favour as well as to dispose at last of the Diamond Necklace.

The de la Mottes engaged the services of an extremely able forger, Villette, who also became Jeanne's lover the more firmly to bind him to their purposes. By the

April of 1784, Jeanne was able to show the Cardinal letters from the Queen, forged by Villette on paper stamped with blue *fleur-de-lys*, which proved to his satisfaction not only that she was deep in Marie Antoinette's confidence but that she had used her influence on his behalf and that the Queen was relenting of her hard treatment of him.

In the July of 1784, the de la Motte ménage was completed by a young mistress whom the Count had taken, Marie Laguay, whom Jeanne (in virtue of her Valois blood) created Baronne Gay d'Oliva (anagramistically, Valoi). Fortunately for them all the 'Baronne' had a distinct resemblance to the Queen.

Before long Jeanne told Gay that the Queen wanted her help in a practical joke, for which she was willing to pay £600. 'You are only asked to give, some evening, a note and a rose to a great lord in an alley in the gardens of Versailles. My husband will take you there.' Gay, apparently, asked for more information for what seemed to be an overpaid service, but, as Jeanne de la Motte noted in her Memoirs: 'It was not very difficult for me to persuade the girl, for she is very stupid.'

And so it came about that, on August 11, 1784, in the Grove of Venus in the gardens of Versailles, under a clouded, heavy sky without moon or star, the Cardinal de Rohan was forgiven by Marie Antoinette—or so he imagined as he knelt and kissed the skirt of her dress and she dropped a rose and said words which he understood to mean that the past was forgiven.

Gay, (who had been dressed by Jeanne de la Motte in a simple white blouse like that worn by Marie Antoinette in the portrait of her by Madame Vigée-Lebrun, which had been exhibited at the Salon of 1783) gave her own account of the proceedings: 'M. and Madame de la Motte took me into the Park. There a rose was put into my hand by Madame de la Motte, who said to me: "You will give this rose and the letter you have to the person who will present himself and say to him these words: 'You know what this means.'

'She accompanied me to a hedge of yoke-elms, leaving me there while she went to fetch the great nobleman to whom I was to speak. It was a dull night, not a speck of moonlight, nor could I discover anything but those persons and objects which were familiar to me. It would be quite impossible for me to describe the state I was in. I was so agitated, so excited, so disconcerted and so tremulous that I cannot conceive how I was able to accomplish even half of what I had been told to do.

'I offered the rose to the great nobleman and said to him: "You know what this means" or something very similar. I cannot say whether he took it or let it fall. As for the letter, it remained in my pocket. I had entirely forgotten it. As soon as I had spoken, Madame de la Motte came running up to us, saying in a low hurried voice: "Quick! Quick! Come away." '

For obvious reasons, Jeanne de la Motte dared not risk any conversation. A sentence or two from Gay would have convinced the Cardinal that she was not the Queen. As it was, he was full of gratitude to the clever and charming and influential Jeanne de la Motte who had had him restored to favour and he was not as surprised as he otherwise might have been when, some months later, she brought him the news that the Queen wanted him to buy the Diamond Necklace for her. The price by now had come down to 1,600,000 livres and the Queen would pay for it in four instalments at intervals of six months—the first 400,000 to fall due in the August of 1785.

The Cardinal, easily impressed as he was, insisted on seeing the Necklace to examine it before he bought it. He remarked, truly enough, that it was in excessively bad taste. He also insisted that the Queen should send him some kind of written guarantee. With Villette the forger at hand, the guarantee was easily forthcoming, with the further information that, bad taste or not, the Queen wanted to wear it at the Candlemas ceremonies on February 2.

So on February 1, 1785, the Cardinal got the Necklace from Böhmer, who was satisfied both with the contract and the information that it was not to be talked about. On the same day, he received a note from the Queen, asking him to be at Jeanne de la Motte's house at Versailles with the casket containing the Necklace.

When he arrived, the Cardinal was slightly surprised that he was not allowed to take it to the Queen himself; but she sent a note saying that the King was with her, that she did not know how long he would stay and that he could safely entrust the casket to the messenger she was sending. He did so and the 'messenger' (who was Villette the forger) delivered the Diamond Necklace to the person who had decided she wanted it. Not that it left the house. But as soon as the Cardinal had, Jeanne de la Motte and her husband cut the Necklace up with a heavy and rather blunt knife. Taking the best stones, the 'Count' crossed to England where, as we have seen, he sold or bartered them for other pieces with Gray of New Bond Street and Jeffreys of Piccadilly. With the proceeds, the de la Mottes, with six carriages and a stud of horses, with silver plate and a superb wardrobe and a dazzling display of jewels went back to Bar-sur-Aube, where Jeanne had once cried: 'Pity a poor orphan of the blood of the Valois!'

Five months went by. The Cardinal wondered why the Queen still did not see him and the jeweller wondered why she never wore the Necklace; but neither of them took any steps until, on July 12, Böhmer decided to send her a tactful note which might remind her that the first instalment would soon be due. The Cardinal dictated the note and when the Queen received it she was very puzzled. She read it aloud to her Lady-in-Waiting: 'Madame, we are extremely happy to think that the last arrangements which have been proposed to us and to which we have submitted with respectful zeal will be received as a new instance of our submission and devotedness to Your Majesty's commands and we feel truly rejoiced to think that the most beautiful set of diamonds in the world will be worn by the best and greatest of Queens. . . . You hear that, Madame Campan?'

'Yes, Your Majesty. What does it mean?'

'I thought as you managed to solve the puzzle in the *Mercure* this morning you might be able to tell me. That madman Böhmer's just sent it to me. You might see him and find out what it means—and tell him I do not require his services any longer.'

And, with that, the Queen twisted the note up and burnt it at a taper which stood alight in her library for sealing letters. Had she not done this, but instead sent for Böhmer there and then and asked him what it meant the whole plot would have been exposed and none but the villains would have been hurt. But she can hardly have been blamed for thinking that Böhmer's monomania about the unsaleable Necklace had at last driven him out of his mind.

It was not until exactly a month later, on August 12, that the Queen extracted from Böhmer (who in the meantime had been told by Jeanne de la Motte that the Queen's guarantee to the Cardinal was a forgery)* all the facts as far as the jeweller knew them; and on August 15—the Feast of the Assumption—just before the Cardinal was about to celebrate at High Mass, the King asked him: 'My cousin, what is this tale of a diamond necklace bought by you in the name of the Queen?'

The Cardinal was so taken aback that he was unable to speak coherently and was allowed to write the story in as short a space as he could. He managed to compress it into fifteen lines which, when the Queen saw them, made her say furiously: 'How could you believe that I, who have not spoken to you for eight years, entrusted you with such a commission?'

The King and Queen, most foolishly, refused the Cardinal's offer to pay for the Necklace in return for the hushing-up of the scandal. Napoleon's comment later exactly expresses the situation: 'The Queen was innocent, and to make her innocence the more public, she wished the Parlement to be the judge. The result was that she was taken to be guilty.'

At the subsequent trial in the January of 1786, the Cardinal was acquitted, though suitable punishments were meted out to such of the others as were within reach—de la Motte himself, it will be remembered, had escaped to England in time—and 'officially' Marie

---

* Her motive here seems to have been the calculation that the Cardinal, to escape scandal, would pay the money himself.

Antoinette's reputation was vindicated. But the populace, inflamed by the revolutionaries, continued to believe that the Cardinal was the Queen's lover, who had stolen the Necklace to please her and that the wicked aristos had put the blame on good defenceless bourgeois like Jeanne de la Motte and Villette and Gay d'Oliva. Of the three, it was Gay who was the most popular. 'Pretty, a young mother and profoundly dissolute, she was the darling of Liberal and *sensible* hearts.'

[iii] The Escape from the Salpêtrière

The escape of Jeanne de la Motte from her imprisonment is best told in her own words, not because her account of it is necessarily more true than any of her other statements but because it is the only one there is; and it is on this statement as a whole, whatever its value, that any solution must be based.

'It was about the latter end of November or the commencement of December, 1786,' she wrote, 'that one of the soldiers doing duty as sentinel in the court of the Salpêtrière, to see that the women made no holes in the dormitory to escape by the aqueducts, passed the end of his musket through a broken part of the wall and attempted to touch Angelica, who waited upon me as a servant and who was sentenced to be confined for life in the Salpêtrière.

' "What do you want with me?" asked Angelica.

' "Is not your name Angelica?" he said softly: "Are you not the person who waits upon Madame de la Motte?"

' "Yes," replied she.

' "Very well," said he. "I heard many lords and ladies in the Palais Royal yesterday mention your name as being the person who is so attentive to her. Tell me if you want anything. I always carry about me an inkstand, paper etc., which I will furnish you with, as I know you have not permission to write. Prepare your letters if you wish to write to anybody and I will take charge of them."

'Angelica thanked him for his kindness, but frankly confessed she could neither read nor write.

' "No matter," replied he. "There is your mistress, Madame de la Motte. I would advise you to get her to write for you to the different ladies who come here and beg her to recommend you to their goodness."

'Two days after this, about three in the morning, the same soldier again touched Angelica with his musket and gave her a packet of gilt paper, a large bundle of quills, a bottle of ink and a letter for herself. "Madame de la Motte will read it to you," said he. Next day Angelica brought me the letter, at every line of which I was struck with such astonishment that I could scarcely believe my eyes. This mysterious letter was as follows: "Assure yourself, Mademoiselle Angelica, that I shall be extremely happy if I can be instrumental in procuring your liberty. Command me and believe that I shall seize every opportunity of being useful to you [and, immediately preceding the last line] *Unfortunate*, put this letter before the light—'*Tis understood*—be sure to be discreet.'

'After having read to Angelica so much of this letter as concerned her, I made use of some pretext to send her to the dormitory, and the moment I was alone put the letter to the light, when writing began to appear as if by the power of magic. At length all was visible and the following words astonished my eyes:

' "You are earnestly exhorted to keep up your spirits and to take proper nourishment that you may have sufficient strength to support the fatigue of your journey. *People* are now intent on changing your condition. Speak your wishes and mention the day you are willing to depart, that a post-chaise may be prepared which you will find at the corner of the King's garden. Be discreet: 'tis your interest to be so. Confide implicitly in the bearer, without entertaining the smallest suspicion.' "

'Judge of my astonishment on perusing this mysterious paper! Surely, said I to myself, I am awake and in sober certainty of the truth of what I see. But who can be the persons who have thus interested themselves in my misfortunes? This singular expression, "It is understood" was never used by any person but myself, the Cardinal and the Queen. Perhaps they both, repenting of what they have done, ashamed of having the weakness to suffer me to be sacrificed, at this moment wish to give me liberty.'

To this letter, Jeanne de la Motte says that she wrote an answer, saying that she was anxious to escape from her confinement and begged her unknown correspondent to aid her in the attempt. In due course, she received the following reply: '*People* have reflected; endeavour to procure the model of the key that will open easily that side where you wish to go out. Act for the best and compose yourself!'

'For two months,' she continued, 'I laboured at the attempt and at length succeeded in making two

designs—one small and the other large—in which I
thought I had fortunately delineated the wards of the
key, and which, the moment I perceived to be perfect,
I enclosed in a letter which I gave to Angelica to convey
to the soldier who, about a fortnight afterwards,
brought a key made exactly after the paper model.*

'I had the patience to wait two whole days without
sufficient resolution to make the experiment; but on
Sunday, between six and seven in the morning, when
Angelica and myself were together in the gallery, the
opportunity seeming favourable, with a trembling hand
and palpitating heart I applied the key to the lock
when, gracious Heaven! what was my surprise and joy
at the finding the door opened! We both endeavoured
as much as possible to conceal our emotions and
proceeded to try whether the same key would open the
other three doors. In the afternoon of the same day I
pulled off my shoes and crept softly along to the second
door, which, to my great joy, was also obsequious to
my touch. I shut it again, ascended the steps softly by
three at a time, all in a tremble for fear of discovery,
and found, as I wished, all was fast and everything quiet.
I then attempted to open the door on the other side of
the gallery near the second dormitory. This I did with
wonderful facility, and with as little trouble as I had
opened the others.'

Angelica was released on May 1 and it is obvious
that, until she was safely out of prison, Jeanne de la
Motte was also unable to leave it. She had—according
to her own account—the necessary key in February;

* I am inclined to agree with Vizetelly who, in his book on the
Diamond Necklace writes: 'We suspect the whole of this key business
to be fudge.'

but she did not actually leave till June. By the hands of Angelica, presumably, or someone whom Angelica had arranged to see her, she sent on May 13 a letter to one of her old lovers, the Baron de Crussol (who had played Basile in the famous production of *The Barber of Seville* when Marie Antoinette had played Rosina). The letter was, in the main, one of her usual appeals for money, but in it she mentioned that the following week the Duchess de Duras, *dame du palais* to the Queen was to pay her a visit. 'I shall see her alone; the public must not know it, as it might get talked about on account of my being forbidden to see anyone for fear I should speak.' Of this visit, there does not seem to be any other confirmation and it sounds intrinsically improbable. The motive of mentioning it to de Crussol would seem to be propagate the pretence that the Queen and the Cardinal were 'relenting' and consequently facilitating her escape.

The narrative continues: 'I reflected within myself that if I should run the hazard of going out in the dress of the Salpêtrière, I should be easily discovered in the event of being met by any of the Sisters. I conceived also that a male habit would be more favourable for my escape and communicated this to my unknown correspondent, to whom I wrote: "I wish to have a large blue coat, a flannel waistcoat, black breeches, a pair of half-boots, a round high-crowned hat to make me appear taller, a switch and a pair of leather gloves.'

'All these the guard brought me about ten or twelve days after; he carried the great-coat under his cloak, the waistcoat in his pocket and the switch in the barrel of his musket; and about two nights after he brought the half-boots and a man's shirt. Thus furnished with wings for my flight, I was wholly intent on my game and, what is not a little singular, without the least fear of not being able to effect my escape. . . . I reflected that I was under the immediate protection of the Queen and would not suffer myself to entertain a doubt that it was the Queen and no one else who had taken this interest in my behalf.

'After a time, however, a feeling of apprehension came across my mind and led me to suspect the sincerity of my unknown correspondent. Surely, I thought to self, this cannot be a plot concerted to lull me to security that I may be more easily got rid of. It cannot be so! They really wish to render me service. There can be doubt of it since I have the key and the proper dress; but whither will this post-chaise conduct me? Probably to some convent; and does the Queen suppose that I can be happy there? I will never consent to go to a convent, and only to some place where I can be free—where I am at liberty!

'About this time I was not a little surprised by a visit from M. de Crosne, Lieutenant of Police. About six o'clock one afternoon I was conducted to Sister Martha's apartment, where I saw M. de Crosne, with M. Martin, secretary, and another person who was a stranger. M. de Crosne at first did not know me; he appeared much surprised and affected to find me so reduced, so altered; and his sensibility deeply affected me. . . . I stood for some moments unable to articulate a single syllable. At length, awaking from my reverie, I saluted him, when the amiable man kindly enquired if there was anything I was in want of as, if so, he would give the necessary orders. At these words I quite lost myself and, forgetting every consideration that should have restrained me, I drew near him and repeated: "Want anything? O, sir, it is too much to bear—that I should be thus confined!" M. de Crosne, greatly affected, would not suffer me to recite the melancholy catalogue of my woes. . . . I could not help thinking that M. de Crosne was sent hither expressly to see me, and the more I reflected upon this visit of him, the more suspicious I became. I began to see that they were fearful I should say too much and that it was judged expedient rather to endeavour to soothe than to drive me to extremities; for if I had really any ill-will, any grudge towards the Queen, I thought to myself, neither the Baron de Breteuil nor the Lieutenant of the Police would take the pains to favour me with the slightest attention.'

At last the final plan was made. One day between June 8 and June 11, at either eleven in the morning or six at night, the guard was to disguise himself as a waggoner and, with a whip in his hand, was to walk round the King's Garden (the Jardin des Plantes). Jeanne de la Motte in her male disguise was to be accompanied by Angelica's successor, Marianne, who knew her way about the prison.

The time eventually chosen was the morning of June 11. The key opened the four doors, as it had done in rehearsal. Though she had lost sight of Marianne, Jeanne de la Motte records: 'I did not lose my courage but passed on until I found myself in a large hall wherein were a great number of small beds in each of which was a child. After having cast my eyes round me, I enquired of the Sisters the way out. I did not well understand the directions they gave me, but, after traversing many courts, found myself at length in a

spacious court among a number of people who had
come to gratify their curiosity by a sight of this prison.
I followed a part who entered the chapel to view it,
taking care to mix myself up with the rest of the
company. After addressing a fervent prayer to Heaven
to inspire me with courage, I soon had the gratification
of finding myself outside those doors which I had always
looked on as impassable. Here I saw no one but the
Sisters, to whom I gave some money as though I were
an ordinary visitor, and at length fortunately·reached
the high road. Here, after some delay, I discovered my
good Marianne waiting for me near the river.'

Eventually she reached Luxembourg where a Mrs
MacMahon met her, on July 27, bringing a note from
her husband in London. With Mrs MacMahon, she
immediately set off for London, where she was reunited
with the 'Count' and with Angelica, who re-entered her
service. At the time it was commonly supposed that
the authorities not only connived at the escape but
abetted it and that, at the moment of departure, the
Superior of the Salpêtrière said jokingly: 'Farewell,
Madame, take great care you are not remarked'
(which meant also re-marked by the branding-iron).
This suggestion, however, merely brings the whole
escape into line with the de la Motte propaganda-
version that the Queen and Cardinal 'relented.' But
as the Queen had nothing to relent of and as she was
now on even worse terms with the Cardinal than she
had been before, finding his presumption the last and
intolerable insult, it is quite impossible that they could
have co-operated in procuring the escape of the one
person it was essential to keep in prison.

On the other hand it was quite clear that Jeanne de

la Motte had powerful friends who, for revolutionary if not for personal reasons, were prepared to help her; and it seems to me that the obliging guard, as well as Angelica and Marianne and Mrs MacMahon may well have played the parts that the Memoir assigns to them. The story, indeed, suggests members of a secret society, (of which, of course, there were many at the time, all intent on, in their own way, fanning the flame of revolution). And, if we accept Jeanne's account of the letters she received as being substantially accurate and the phrasing such as the Cardinal and only the Cardinal was accustomed to use, then there is an obvious and even inescapable clue pointing to one person—Cagliostro.

[iv] Cagliostro

'That unutterable business of the Diamond Necklace!' writes Carlyle. 'Red-hatted Cardinal Louis de Rohan; Sicilian jailbird Balsamo Cagliostro; milliner Dame de Lamotte "with a face of some piquancy"; the highest Church Dignitaries waltzing, in Walpurgis Dance, with quack-prophets, pick-purses and public women—a whole Satan's Invisible World Displayed!'

'Jail-bird Balsamo,' 'quack-prophet' and, usually 'Charlatan' or even 'Prince of Charlatans'—these are the epithets conventionally applied to Cagliostro which, though true, tend to obscure the real nature of the man. His name was indeed Balsamo; he was several times in prison and died in one; he indulged, since his public wanted it and was infinitely credulous, in quack-prophecy and charlatanry. Yet that façade was of his own choosing. It hid his true motives and intentions.

And it is difficult not to think that it was deliberately assumed for purposes of safety, as Hamlet assumed his madness.

Joseph Balsamo was the son of a tradesman in Palermo, where he was born in 1743. (He derived the name Cagliostro from a great uncle.) In his early youth he belonged to a religious order—the Brothers of Charity. He was remarkable for his intelligence and his brilliance in the study of medicine. He became a practising alchemist and when he was about thirty came into contact with the Illuminati who thought, correctly, that he would be an admirable missionary for their doctrines. He was initiated in a cave not far from Frankfort, when for the first time he discovered that the real object of this powerful secret society was to overturn the thrones of Europe and that the first blow was to fall in France. He also found that the society had enormous funds, subscribed by its members, which were invested in the banks of Amsterdam, Rotterdam, Basle, Lyons, London, Venice and Genoa. A considerable sum of money was placed at his own disposal (which he later pretended he had 'made' alchemically) to propagate in France the disruptive doctrines of the sect. It was on this mission that he first visited Strasbourg in 1780, when he adopted for his device L.P.D., meaning *Lilia pedibus destrue* (Trample the lilies under foot).

He was probably a hypnotist, certainly a physician, who healed the poor without charge and thereby gained an enormous (and deserved) popularity among the masses, which further served his real aims. He was an adept at alchemy, knew something of natural magic and was an enthusiastic Freemason. One who met him

thus described him: 'Cagliostro was anything but handsome; still I have never seen a more remarkable
physiognomy; above all, he had a penetrating look
which seemed almost supernatural. I know not how to
describe the impression of his eyes; it was at once fire
and ice; attracted and repelled you at the same time;
made you afraid and inspired you with an irrepressible
curiosity. One might draw two different portraits of
him, both resembling him and yet totally dissimilar.'

This remarkable man entirely dominated the Cardinal
de Rohan and was intimate with the de la Mottes. He
arrived in Paris just at the time the Cardinal was making
the final arrangements for the purchase of the Necklace.

He was tried, but acquitted, for a share in the affair.
He was, however, told to leave France and, in the June
of 1786 went to England where he remained for two
years. In 1789, after the Revolution had broken out in
France, he went to Rome (which was the city next on
the list of the Illuminati) where he fell into the hands of
the authorities and, after a trial by the Inquisition, was
condemned as a leading member of the Illuminati and
died in prison in 1795.

During the time that Jeanne de la Motte was escaping
from the Salpêtrière, Cagliostro was safely in London
and in touch with de la Motte. With his wide 'secret
society' contacts in France and with boundless money
at his disposal for organization and bribes, it would be
stranger if he were not the organizer of the escape, (the
result of which so notably helped his cause), than if he
were. All the people involved—the guard, the women,
the 'friends at Court,' Mrs MacMahon—fit into that
pattern; and by his intimate knowledge of the Cardinal
and his conduct of the Necklace affair, he would be

able to send the right kind of messages to Jeanne de la Motte in prison.

On the other hand, as he and she had publicly quarrelled when at the trial he had brought to earth her fantasies about a *seance* he had once arranged, he would not let her know that he was the mysterious benefactor. She, whose friendship had turned quickly to the hate that is born of wounded pride, called him a 'low empiric' and determined to revenge herself on him. But it is clear that he was not of a nature which would let personalities stand in the way of his grand design; and the purpose of the Illuminati would be best served by having Jeanne de la Motte in England where she could safely write and publish the calumnies which were to be the final fuel to kindle the revolutionary flame.

That the clue to the enigma of the escape is Cagliostro —not the 'charlatan' but the real Cagliostro with his convictions and his underground army—I have personally no doubt; and I hope that one day a Frenchman will reconsider the whole of the Diamond Necklace affair with him in mind. It might well be that the 'Charlatan' would then be found to play anything but the subsidiary and rather comic role now assigned to him. I should not be surprised if he were the ruthless originator of the whole plot.

Unexpectedly on the spot, Cryer cleared his throat, playing for time. 'Me, sir?'

'Yes. Quinnan for a commendation?'

'Sergeant Penny wasn't too happy about him cutting corners and chasing things off his own bat, without a word to any of us.'

'Can't say I approve of that sort of thing myself,' said Brownlow piously. 'We've discussed it before, haven't we, Derek?'

Conway managed a stiff nod. 'We have indeed, sir.'

'But it did get a result. What a result!'

Bob Cryer said: 'It really was a sharp piece of thinking, sir. You'd have no trouble getting it approved.'

'Provided Blake's convicted,' said Monroe sharply.

'Same applies in the case of recommending the arresting officer, sir.'

'True.' Brownlow made his choice. 'Quinnan's young and presentable. We'll go with him, I think. "Meritorious alertness and use of initiative" – something like that. Thank you.' As Cryer, taking this as the end of the discussion, was about to move off, Brownlow added with a boisterousness that rang hideously out of tune: 'Just don't let Blake escape. Or kill himself.'

Tom Penny let himself out into the yard and drew a deep breath. He could not control it: the breath shuddered, and his chest shuddered and he thought he might throw up against the nearest vehicle.

He half collapsed against the side wall, then forced himself to stand up. His eyes felt hazed. He could see nothing, and wanted to see nothing. His whole inside was scoured, and his mind had been left with nothing but a coating of filth and fear. Inevitably he would be asked for an official report; and he did not know how he was going to find the words to put down, cold and sober and matter-of-fact.

Dave Quinnan came swaggering out, letting the door swing shut behind him.

191

'Back in his hutch, is he, sarge?'

'Yeah. Back in his hutch.'

'Such an ordinary-looking little nerd. Never know what goes on in people's minds, do you? Still,' said Quinnan breezily, 'it's done me no harm.'

'Good.' Penny was not really listening.

Quinnan patted his arm with a familiarity that would normally have produced a snarl of outrage. 'Tell you about it later, sarge.'

Penny gazed out across the station yard. Ordinary, everyday things were coming back into focus. Such as Burnside stomping in his usual way towards his car and driving out with an unnecessary roar from the exhaust. And such as Viv Martella walking towards another car and opening the back door. Behind her came an ordinary sort of woman in an ordinary, inexpensive coat, leading a black and white Border collie. It was all of it so ordinary, so normal.

Penny watched remotely as Martella drove off into the outside world. Sooner or later he would have to get back into that world himself.